Primer of

Experimental Poetry 1

1870-1922

Primer of

Experimental Poetry 1

1870-1922

edited by
EDWARD LUCIE-SMITH

rapp+
whiting
André
Deutsch

FIRST PUBLISHED 1971 BY
RAPP AND WHITING LIMITED
105 GREAT RUSSELL STREET LONDON WC 1

PRINTED IN GREAT BRITAIN BY
BILLING & SONS LIMITED
GUILDFORD AND LONDON

ISBN 0 85391 118 5

Acknowledgments

Acknowledgement is made to the following who have kindly granted permission to reprint some of the poems included in this volume:

Verlag Helmut Küpper for 'Franken' by Stefan George from *Der Siebente Ring* and Random House Inc., for the translation, 'Frankish Lands', from *Poems* by Stefan George, translated by Carol North Valhope and Ernst Morwitz, copyright © 1943 by Pantheon Books, a division of Random House, Inc. Insel Verlag for 'Die Erste Elegie' by Rainer Maria Rilke from *Duineser Elegien*, and the Hogarth Press Ltd., St. John's College, Oxford, Mr. Stephen Spender and W. W. Norton & Co. Inc. (copyright © 1939 by W. W. Norton & Co. Inc., copyright renewed 1967 by Stephen Spender and J. B. Leishman), for the translation, 'The First Elegy', from the *Duino Elegies*, translated by Stephen Spender and J. B. Leishman. The Bobbs–Merrill Co. Inc. and MacGibbon & Kee Ltd. for the translations of 'The Warmth' by Benedict Konstantinovich Livshits, 'We lift the heavens, the heavens by the ears . . .' by Anatoly Borisovich Marienhof, 'Incantation by Laughter' by Velemir Khlebnikov, and 'Heights' by Aleksei Eliseyevich Kruchonykh, all from *Modern Russian Poetry*, edited by Vladimir Markov and Merrill Sparks. Les Éditions Denoël for 'Dernière heure' and 'Natures Mortes' by Blaise Cendrars from *Du monde entier*. Librairie Ernest Flammarion for 'L'Ombre du mur' by Pierre Reverdy from *Plupart du temps* and Mr. Keith Bosley for his translation, 'The Shadow of the Wall'. Yale University Press for 'Bee Time Vine' by Gertrude Stein from *Bee Time Vine and Other Pieces (1913–1927)*, copyright © 1953 by Alice B. Toklas. Editions Gallimard for 'Les Fenêtres' and 'Il Pleut' by Guillaume Apollinaire from *Calligrammes d'Apollinaire*, 'La Douche' by Jean Cocteau from *Poésies 1916–1923*, and 'Madame Tussaud's' by Valéry Larbaud from *Poésies de A. O. Barnabooth*; and Mr. Roger Shattuck for his translation of Apollinaire's 'Les Fenêtres'; Editions Gallimard and Calder & Boyars Ltd.

5

Acknowledgments

Corporation for the translation by Donald D. Walsh from *An Anthology of Contemporary Latin–American Poetry* edited by Dudley Fitts, copyright © 1942, 1947 by New Directions Publishing Corporation. Faber & Faber Ltd. and New Directions Publishing Corporation for 'Salutation the Second' by Ezra Pound from *Personæ*, © 1926 by Ezra Pound.

Contents

Contents

Introduction

In the review of James Joyce's *Dubliners* which he published in *The Egoist* in July 1914, Ezra Pound attacked the idea of 'impressionist' writing, or, rather, of writing which strove to imitate the effects of the Impressionist painters. At the same time, however, he made handsome acknowledgement of the fact that there was some subterranean link between all the arts, whose presence could be detected in literature as well as in painting:

> The spirit of a decade strikes properly upon all of the arts. There are 'parallel movements'. Their causes and their effects may not seem, superficially, similar.
>
> This mimicking of painting ten or twenty years late, is not the least the same as the 'literary movement' parallel to the painting movement imitated.
>
> The force that leads a poet to leave out a moral reflection may lead a painter to leave out representation. The resultant poem may not suggest the resultant painting.

Pound at that time evidently thought that the heady excitements of modernism were in some danger of blinding people to the fact that literature established its own rules, which could not be precisely those of painting, however closely the painters and writers might live together.

At the present time, more than half a century after Pound wrote the words I have quoted, there seems to be an opposite danger. The study of modern painting and the study of modern literature are now such separate disciplines, especially among those whose native tongue is English, that the close connection between literary modernist and the innovators in the visual arts is in danger of being ignored and forgotten. Sometimes, indeed, it turns out that the modern poets and the modern artists were the same people. Dada was just as much a literary movement as one which concerned itself with the visual arts. It is the purpose of this book to illustrate, in schematic form, the nature of the connection I have mentioned.

In many ways, it has a greater resemblance to a book about modern art than it has to a book about modern literature. It is international. It attempts to deal, in outline, with the ethos of a whole period. It ignores language-barriers so far as it can conveniently do so.

Obviously, in view of its size, it is not—and was never intended to be—a comprehensive anthology. The day for that may come later. In fact, it is hardly to be thought of as an anthology at all, but rather as a textbook with illustrations— the most salient examples I could find to clarify my ideas. Many famous names which belong to the period 1870-1922 are missing from it—they range from Anna Akhmatova to W. B. Yeats. I have not chosen what I believe to be the greatest poems of the epoch, but rather those which serve to illustrate a particular argument.

Before embarking upon these arguments, it would perhaps be helpful to say something about the nature of the book as a whole. One excuse for writing it is simply that there is remarkably little information to be found on the subject. Almost the only well-informed treatment of the relationship between modern painting and modern poetry that I know is to be found in L. Moholy-Nagy's book *Vision in Motion* (Paul Theobald & Co., Wheaton, Ill., 1961). The chapter is too brief, and deals chiefly with the Dadaists. Significantly enough, while the book is a well-known textbook in art colleges, it is scarcely ever mentioned by literary critics.

My treatment of the subject covers a broader spectrum of writers and a longer period of time than Moholy-Nagy attempted to deal with. One of my chief difficulties lay in knowing where to begin. It seems clear that the modernist spirit can be discerned earlier in literature, and especially in French literature, than it can in painting. When Baudelaire discusses the drawings of Constantin Guys in *Le Peintre de la vie moderne* what he writes seems to reveal an eye and a sensibility which are much more advanced than those of the artist himself.

Take, for example, Baudelaire's remarks about Guys's rapid notations of carriages as they bowled along:

> The pleasure that the artist's eye obtains is derived, so it seems, from the series of geometrical figures that the object in question— of itself so complicated, whether ship or coach—successively and rapidly creates in space.

Painting did not really arrive at this particular stage of perception until the experiments of Robert Delaunay and of the Italian Futurists, such as Giacomo Ballà and Umberto Boccioni.

What is especially striking is the way in which Baudelaire, even at this early date, seizes upon characteristics which were afterwards to fascinate revolutionaries in the visual arts. When he speaks of 'geometrical figures . . . in space', for example, he is already adumbrating the principles of abstract art, and giving some idea of how abstraction was arrived at. His use of the adverbs 'successively' and 'rapidly' is also significant, as we have here the first hint of the principle of simultaneity, which was to mean so much to Cubists and Futurists alike.

1. Symbolism

The Symbolist poets and the Impressionist painters in France were linked by important friendships—notably that between Mallarmé and Manet. In a general sense, they had certain aims in common. Often, it was the artist's as well as the poet's desire to convey a purely aesthetic sensation, divorced from subject-matter: a pattern of light on the retina, a pattern of words in the mind. The existence of painters who can properly be called Symbolists, such as Odilon Redon, does, however, make it plain that the Impressionist painters pursued a somewhat different line of exploration from that chosen by their poetic contemporaries. Symbolism was gradually, as the nineteenth century waned, to increase its hold upon the visual arts. Gauguin and the whole Pont-Aven Group were heavily influenced by Symbolist doctrine, and since their work, in turn, was the direct ancestor of that of the Fauves, it is clear that Symbolism was a source for 'modernist' ideas in a general sense, as well as the movement which produced the first poems which are still, to the men of the mid-twentieth century, 'modern'.

I have chosen to represent five poets among my examples. Three are French and two are German. Arthur Rimbaud was classified by Verlaine as a *poète maudit* rather than as a Symbolist. The prose-poem 'Villes II', is from the sequence *Les Illuminations*, which seems to have been written between 1873 and 1875, during travels in Belgium, England and Germany. The title of the series is an anglicism, and means 'coloured illustrations'. In *Les Illuminations* Rimbaud is deliberately transposing his experience, as the painters were later to transpose theirs; he has consciously assumed the role of seer or *voyant*, which painters, too, were later to claim.

'Villes II' seems to me an especially interesting text for my purposes because it embodies two of the major themes which are to be recognized in 'modernist' poetry—that of the city, and that of dislocation. Indeed, the urban panorama, where the parts are deliberately dislocated and do not quite fit together, is what the poet is at pains to create for us. The imagery is eclectic, and the details are drawn from different periods and places. The main sources, however, seem to be the illustrations of such men as 'Mad' Martin and Gustave Doré. Though the form is that of the prose-poem, the writing itself has little to do with prose-logic. The last sentence offers an especially interesting ambiguity, in the use of the word 'chroniques', which can either be taken as the 'chronicles' of the Middle Ages, or the 'newspapers' of today. The final phrase 'la lumière qu'on a créée' is again subtly ambiguous, as it implies not only that the light is in some way artificial rather than natural, but that the poet himself has invented it, together with the poem.

The nature of the poet, and his relationship to what he writes, is the theme of Mallarmé's famous sonnet, 'Le Tombeau d'Edgar Poe'. This was written in 1875 or 1876. Mallarmé translated Poe's own poems into French—Baudelaire had already done the prose. The American poet was one of the major influences upon French poetry of the later nineteenth century. Commemorating him, Mallarmé makes one of his major statements about the absoluteness of art, and the way in which it transcends the imperfections of the artist (in this case Poe's drunkenness). Taken as a whole, the sonnet is a good, though not extreme, example of Mallarmé's deliberately elliptical syntax, which forces the reader to struggle to apprehend the meaning—we have here the beginning of the idea that a work of art ought in some way to *resist* the spectator: the Cubists were perhaps the first to apply it to painting.

The inclusion of 'L'Hiver qui vient', the first poem of Jules Laforgue's *Derniers Vers* (written in 1886) will not perhaps come as a surprise to those who recall T. S. Eliot's often acknowledged debt to him. Eliot said that Laforgue was 'if not quite the greatest French poet after Baudelaire . . . certainly the most important single technical innovator'. Laforgue himself was hostile to talk of reasons and explanations—his contribution was to shatter still further the idea of prose-logic in poetry, and to substitute for it a way of writing which was modelled upon the procedures of the musician. At the same time, he extended the boundaries of verse to include not only the surprising metaphors and tropes which Eliot imitated from him, but low and slangy words as well as deliberately poetic ones. The skill of his manipulation of diction really depends on the sensitivity of his ear not only to rhythm, but to clashes and contrasts of tone. He himself once said: 'When will we show ourselves to be adequate to the value of phenomena and when will we live with the right tone?' To Rimbaud's notion of the seer or *voyant*, Laforgue therefore added that of the poet as the possessor of a special and elusive tone of voice, which could be embodied in words but scarcely explained by them. It is interesting to note that Laforgue translated Whitman, just as Mallarmé translated Poe. The two great American poets of the nineteenth century are, together with Baudelaire, the ancestors of modernism.

Symbolism proved a viable creed in a wide variety of languages. The last great Symbolist master, W. B. Yeats, died in 1939. The Russian Acmeist (Acmeism owed much to Symbolism) Anna Akhmatova, died more recently still. But, while Symbolism remained a kind of norm for poets who had broken away from the traditions of the nineteenth century—all, that is, except Symbolism itself—modernism was to go much beyond the basic Symbolist experiment.

The poem 'Franken', by the German poet Stefan George (first published in 1907) specially acknowledges the debt which at least one German poet felt to the French Symbolists, though the style is more 'open' than that of Mallarmé. 'The Frankish Lands' referred to are those of the old Carolingian Empire, which included both Germany and France. This the poet regards as his own native land.

Also usually classified as a Symbolist is the greatest German writer of the period, Rainer Maria Rilke, who was also very much influenced by French culture. He served for a time as the secretary of the sculptor Auguste Rodin, and even wrote poems in French as well as in German. The dramatic birth of the First Duino Elegy has often been narrated. Rilke was staying alone at Schloss Duino on the Adriatic, the property of his friend and patron Princess Marie von Thurn und Taxis. It was January 1912, and a strong wind was blowing. The poet had just received an annoying business letter. He walked up and down outside the castle, wondering how to answer it, and suddenly heard a voice call the first line to him through the roaring of the wind. The rest of the poem followed almost immediately, though Rilke was not to finish the sequence of the Duino Elegies until after the war.

It is, of course, fascinating to discover that a work of the technical elaboration and intellectual complexity of the First Duino Elegy should have been composed, so to speak, *d'un seul coup*. More interesting still is the fact that the way in which the poem was written conformed both to a very ancient, and again to a specifically modern, pattern. The experience which Rilke describes is very much like that kind of visionary possession which is traditional for the shaman, or poet-priest of a nomad tribe. I owe this insight to Bruce Chatwin, who has made a special study of shamanism. The shaman often suffers a visionary crisis when approaching middle-age, somewhere about the age of forty. Rilke was just thirty-six. Rilke was among the earliest of the moderns to lay claim to an experience resembling that of the shaman's, and at the same time, at least by implication, to the shaman's role in society. Rimbaud preceded him in this, as he preceded so many writers in so many other things.

The claim to inspiration, or special knowledge, by its very nature immune to the weapons of critical theory, is one which has been repeatedly made by poets during the past hundred years or so, often to the violent indignation of professional critics. The gradual development of critical theory has been accompanied by an increasing tendency to reject criticism as irrelevant.

In the rest of this book I shall on the whole discuss theories of literature which poets involved in the modern movement have themselves adopted. But it must never be forgotten that theory itself has often been cast aside in favour of the claim to have written a given work while 'out of oneself', in an inspired condition. Such claims were not generally made by painters until the birth of Abstract Expressionism in the mid-1940s.

Editor's Note: It might be helpful to the reader to bear in mind that in *Frankish Lands* by Stefan George (pp. 34-5) a more literal rendering of line 20: 'Im taumel aller dinge die mir teuer' might be 'In the whirl of all the things I cherish'.

L'acropole officielle outre les conceptions de la barbarie moderne les plus colossales. Impossible d'exprimer le jour mat produit par le ciel immuablement gris, l'éclat impérial des bâtisses, et la neige éternelle du sol. On a reproduit dans un goût d'énormité singulier toutes les merveilles classiques de l'architecture. J'assiste à des expositions de peinture dans des locaux vingt fois plus vastes qu'Hampton-Court. Quelle peinture! Un Nabuchodonosor norwégien a fait construire les escaliers des ministères; les subalternes que j'ai pu voir sont déjà plus fiers que des brahmanes, et j'ai tremblé à l'aspect des gardiens de colosses et officiers de constructions. Par le groupement des bâtiments, en squares, cours et terrasses fermées, on a évincé les cochers. Les parcs représentent la nature primitive travaillée par un art superbe. Le haut quartier a des parties inexplicables: un bras de mer, sans bateaux, roule sa nappe de grésil bleu entre des quais chargés de candélabres géants. Un pont court conduit à une poterne immédiatement sous le dôme de la Sainte-Chapelle. Ce dôme est une armature d'acier artistique de quinze mille pieds de diamètre environ.

Sur quelques points des passerelles de cuivre, des plates-formes, des escaliers qui contournent les halles et les piliers, j'ai cru pouvoir juger la profondeur de la ville! C'est le prodige dont je n'ai pas pu me rendre compte: quels sont les niveaux des autres quartiers sur ou sous l'acropole? Pour l'étranger de notre temps la reconnaissance est impossible. Le quartier commerçant est un circus d'un seul style, avec galeries à arcades. On ne voit pas de boutiques, mais la neige de la chaussée est écrasée; quelque nababs, aussi rares que les promeneurs d'un matin de dimanche à Londres, se dirigent vers une diligence de diamants. Quelques divans de velours rouge: on sert des boissons polaires dont le prix varie de huit cents à huit mille roupies. A l'idée de chercher des théâtres sur ce circus, je me réponds que les boutiques doivent contenir des drames assez sombres? Je pense qu'il y a une police; mais

The official acropolis surpasses the hugest conceptions of modern barbarism. Impossible to convey in words the flat light which comes from the unchangingly grey sky, the imperial glitter of the buildings, the eternal snow on the ground. All the classic wonders of architecture have been reproduced, with a strange taste for the gigantic. I saw exhibitions of painting in places twenty times larger than Hampton Court. And what paintings! A Norwegian Nebuchadnezzar had built the stairways of the ministries; the underlings I saw there were already prouder than brahmins, and I trembled at the sight of the guardians of the colossi and the building officials. The cab-drivers have been ousted by grouping the buildings into squares, courtyards and closed-off terraces. The parks display the wildness of nature achieved with wonderful art. The upper part of the city has inexplicable features: an inlet of the sea, with no boats, spreads a sheet of blue sleet between wharves laden with gigantic candelabra. A short bridge leads to a postern immediately beneath the dome of the Sainte-Chapelle. This dome is an artistic framework of steel, some fifteen thousand feet in diameter.

From certain view-points on the copper footbridges, the platforms and staircases which surrounded the market-halls and pillars, I thought I might be able to estimate the depth of the city. But the marvel I was unable to judge was that of the levels of the other parts above or below the acropolis. For the foreigner of our own day, exploration is impossible. The business-quarter is a circus built in uniform style, with arcaded galleries. No shops are visible, but the snow on the roadway is trodden down; a few nabobs, rare as strollers on a Sunday morning in London, are moving towards a diamond coach. A few lounging-places of red velvet: they serve iced drinks at prices between eight hundred and eight thousand rupees. I think of looking for theatres in this circus, and say to myself that the shops must contain dramas which are gloomy enough. I believe the place must have a police-force, but the law must be so odd

23

la loi doit être tellement étrange, que je renonce à me faire une idée des aventuriers d'ici.

Le faubourg, aussi élégant qu'une belle rue de Paris, est favorisé d'un air de lumière; l'élément démocratique compte quelques cents âmes. Là encore, les maisons ne se suivent pas; le faubourg se perd bizarrement dans la campagne, le 'Comté' qui remplit l'occident éternel des forêts et des plantations prodigieuses où les gentilshommes sauvages chassent leurs chroniques sous la lumière qu'on a créée.

1873-5

that I give up trying to imagine what the rogues are like here. A suburb, elegant as a fine street in Paris, is blessed with a shining atmosphere; the democratic element numbers a few hundred. There too, the houses are not regularly built; the suburb melts strangely into the countryside, that 'Shire' which fills the eternal west with forests and prodigious plantations, where barbarous squires hunt their histories under the invented light.

1873-5

Translated by
Edward Lucie-Smith

LE TOMBEAU D'EDGAR POE: Stéphane Mallarmé

Tel qu'en Lui-même enfin l'éternité le change,
Le Poète suscite avec un glaive nu
Son siècle épouvanté de n'avoir pas connu
Que la mort triomphait dans cette voix étrange!

Eux, comme un vil sursaut d'hydre oyant jadis l'ange
Donner un sens plus pur aux mots de la tribu
Proclamèrent trés haut le sortilège bu
Dans le fot sans honneur de quelque noir mélange

Du sol et de la nue hostiles, ô grief!
Si notre idée ne sculpte un bas-relief
Dont la tombe de Poe éblouissante s'orne

Calme bloc ici-bas chu d'un désastre obscur
Que ce granit du moins montre à jamais sa borne
Aux noirs vols du Blasphème épars dans le futur.

1875 or 1876

THE TOMB OF EDGAR POE: Stéphane Mallarmé

Such as into Himself at last Eternity changes him,
The Poet arouses with a naked sword
His age over-awed not to have known
That death was triumphing in this strange voice:

But they, in a vile writhing of an hydra hearing once more
     the Angel
Giving a purer meaning to the words of the tribe,
Proclaimed aloud the charmed potion drunk
In the honourless flood of some dark mixture.

O struggle of the hostile earth and ether!
If with it my idea does not carve a bas-relief
Wherewith Poe's dazzling tomb adorns itself,

Calm block here fallen from an obscure disaster,
Let this granite at least display their bound forever
To the black flights of Blasphemy scattered in the future.

1875 or 1876

Translated by
Edward Lucie-Smith

Editor's Note: This version is based on Mallarmé's own translation into English of a slightly earlier text of the same poem, published in an American magazine. The poet gave the following meanings to some of the phrases:

'naked sword' means when the words take on their absolute value in death. 'This strange voice' is the poet's own voice. 'The Angel' is the poet. Lines 7–8 are meant to signify that the poet was charged with always being drunk. 'Dazzling' means with the idea of such a bas-relief. 'Blasphemy' means blasphemy against poets, such as the charge of Poe being drunk.

L'HIVER QUI VIENT: Jules Laforgue

Blocus sentimental! Messageries du Levant!...
Oh, tombée de la pluie! Oh, tombée de la nuit!
Oh, le vent!...
La Toussaint, la Noël et la Nouvelle Année,
Oh, dans les bruines, toutes mes cheminées!...
D'usines...

On ne peut plus s'asseoir, tous les bancs sont mouillés;
Crois-moi, c'est bien fini jusqu'à l'année prochaine,
Tant les bancs sont mouillés, tant les bois sont rouillés,
Et tant les cors ont fait ton ton, ont fait ton taine!...

Ah! nuées accourues des côtes de la Manche,
Vous nous avez gâté notre dernier dimanche!

Il bruine;
Dans la forêt mouillée, les toiles d'araignées
Ploient sous les gouttes d'eau, et c'est leur ruine.

Soleils plénipotentiaires des travaux en blonds Pactoles
Des spectacles agricoles,
Où êtes-vous ensevelis?
Ce soir un soleil fichu gît au haut du côteau,
Gît sur le flanc, dans les genêts, sur son manteau,
Un soleil blanc comme un crachat d'estaminet
Sur une litière de jaunes genêts,
De jaunes genêts d'automne.
Et les cors lui sonnent!
Qu'il revienne...
Qu'il revienne à lui!
Taïaut! Taïaut! et hallali!
O triste antienne, as-tu fini!...
Et font les fous!...
Et il gît là, comme une glande arrachée dans un cou,
Et il frissonne, sans personne!...

Sentimental blockade! steam-packets from the Levant! ...
O the rain falling! the night falling!
O the wind! ...
All Saints, Christmas, and the New Year,
And, O, all my chimneys in the drizzle! ...
My factory-chimneys ...

We can't sit down any more, the benches are soaked;
Believe me, it's over until next year,
The benches so wet now and the leaves blighted,
And all those horns have gone tally-ho, tantivy, tantivy! ...

Ah! clouds come up from the Channel shores,
You've spoilt our last Sunday!

It's drizzling;
In the wet woods, the spiders' webs
Give way under the drops, the water ruins them.

Plenipotentiary suns of the labours in blond Pactoluses
Of agricultural shows,
Where have they buried you?
This evening a poor sun lies at the height of the hill,
Lies on his side, on his coat, amid the broom,
A sun white as bar-room spittle
Upon a litter of yellow broom,
The yellow broom of autumn.
And the horns sound for him!
Let him come back ...
Let him come back to himself!
Tantivy! tantivy! and view-halloo!
O sad anthem are you done now! ...
And they play the fool! ...
And he lies there, like a gland torn out of a neck,
And he shivers, with no one there! ...

Allons, allons, et hallali!
C'est l'Hiver bien connu qui s'amène;
Oh! les tournants des grandes routes,
Et sans petit Chaperon Rouge qui chemine! ...
Oh! leurs ornières des chars de l'autre mois,
Montant en don quichottesques rails
Vers les patrouilles des nuées en déroute
Que le vent malmène vers les transatlantiques bercails! ...
Accélérons, accélérons, c'est la saison bien connue, cette fois.

Et le vent, cette nuit, il en a fait de belles!
O dégâts, ô nids, ô modestes jardinets!
Mon cœur et mon sommeil: ô échos des cognées! ...

Tous ces rameaux avaient encor leurs feuilles vertes,
Les sous-bois ne sont plus qu'un fumier de feuilles mortes;
Feuilles, folioles, qu'un bon vent vous emporte
Vers les étangs par ribambelles,
Ou pour le feu du garde-chasse,
Ou les sommiers des ambulances
Pour les soldats loin de la France.

C'est la saison, c'est la saison, la rouille envahit les masses,
La rouille ronge en leurs spleens kilométriques
Les fils télégraphiques des grandes routes où nul ne passe.

Les cors, les cors, les cors—mélancoliques! ...
Mélancoliques! ...
S'en vont, changeant de ton,
Changeant de ton et de musique,
Ton ton, ton taine, ton ton! ...
Les cors, les cors, les cors! ...
S'en sont allés au vent du Nord.

Je ne puis quitter ce ton: que d'échos! ...

On, on, and tally-ho!
It's familiar winter turning up;
O! the turnings upon the highroads,
And no Little Red Riding Hood travelling there! . . .
O, their month-old cart-ruts,
Going up in quixotic rails
To the routed cloud-patrols
That the wind rough-houses to the transatlantic sheepfolds! . . .
Faster, faster, o now it's the familiar season.

And the wind, tonight, has done its work well.
O havoc, o nests, o chaste garden-plots!
My heart and my sleep: o echoes of the axe! . . .

All these branches still had their green leaves,
Now the underwoods are just a compost of dead leaves;
Leaves, folioles, may a good wind carry you off
In swarms to the ponds,
Or for the game-keeper's fire,
Or the ambulance mattresses
Of soldiers a long way from France.

The season, the season is come, the blight invades the masses,
The rust eats into the kilometric spleens
Of the telegraph-wires by the highways where nobody goes.

The horns, the horns—the melancholy horns! . . .
Melancholy horns! . . .
Departing, changing their tone,
Changing their tone and their music,
Halloo, lan lone, halloo! . . .
The horns, horns, horns! . . .
Off to the North Wind!

I can't change my tone: what echoes! . . .

C'est la saison, c'est la saison, adieu vendanges! ...
Voici venir les pluies d'une patience d'ange,
Adieu vendanges, et adieu tous les paniers,
Tous les paniers Watteau des bourrées sous les marronniers,
C'est la toux dans les dortoirs du lycée qui rentre,
C'est la tisane sans le foyer,
La phtisie pulmonaire attristant le quartier,
Et toute la misère des grands centres.

Mais, lainages, caoutchoucs, pharmacie, rêve,
Rideaux écartés du haut des balcons des grèves
Devant l'océan de toitures des faubourgs,
Lampes, estampes, thé, petits-fours,
Serez-vous pas mes seules amours! ...
(Oh! et puis, est-ce que tu connais, outre les pianos,
Le sobre et vespéral mystère hebdomadaire
Des statistiques sanitaires
Dans les journaux?)

Non, non! c'est la saison et la planète falote!
Que l'autan, que l'autan
Effiloche les savates que le Temps se tricote!
C'est la saison, Oh déchirements! c'est la saison!
Tous les ans, tous les ans,
J'essaierai en chœur d'en donner la note.

1886

The season, the season is come, good-bye to you vine-
 harvests! . . .
Here come downpours to try the patience of an angel,
Farewell to you vine-harvests, all you baskets good-bye,
All you Watteau panniers that danced under the chestnuts,
Now it's coughing in the dormitories as school-term begins,
Tisanes but no home,
Pulmonary consumption saddening the district,
And all the wretchedness of great cities.

But woollens, rubbers, medicines, dreams,
Curtains drawn back high on balconies, shores
Facing the ocean of suburban roof-tops,
Lamps, stamps, tea, petits fours,
Aren't you my only loves! . . .
(O! then do you know, besides the pianos,
The sober and vesperal weekly mystery
Of the statistics of births and deaths
In the newspapers?)

No, no, the season is come and the planet dims!
May stormy winds from the south, the south,
Unravel the slippers which Time is knitting himself!
The season is come, things rend, the season is come!
Every year, every year,
I shall try in chorus to render its note.

Translated by
Edward Lucie-Smith

1886

B

33

Es war am schlimmsten kreuzweg meiner fahrt:
Dort aus dem abgrund züngelnd giftige flammen,
Hier die gemiednen gaue wo der ekel
Mir schwoll vor allem was man pries und übte,
Ich ihrer und sie meiner götter lachten.
Wo ist dein dichter, arm und prahlend volk?
Nicht einer ist hier: Dieser lebt verwiesen
Und Jenem weht schon frost ums wirre haupt.

Da lud von Westen märchenruf . . . so klang
Das lob des ahnen seiner ewig jungen
Grossmütigen erde deren ruhm ihn glühen
Und not auch fern ihn weinen liess, der mutter
Der fremden unerkannten und verjagten . . .
Ein rauschen bot dem erben gruss als lockend
In freundlichkeit und fülle sich die ebnen
Der Maas und Marne unterm frühlicht dehnten.

Und in der heitren anmut stadt, der gärten
Wehmütigem reiz, bei nachtbestrahlten türmen
Verzauberten gewölbs umgab mich jugend
Im taumel aller dinge die mir teuer—
Da schirmten held und sänger das Geheimnis:
VILLIERS sich hoch genug für einen thron,
VERLAINE in fall und busse fromm und kindlich
Und für sein denkbild blutend: MALLARMÉ.

Mag traum und ferne uns als speise stärken—
Luft die wir atmen bringt nur der Lebendige.
So dank ich freunde euch die dort noch singen
Und väter die ich seit zur gruft geleitet . . .
Wie oft noch spät da ich schon grund gewonnen
In trüber heimat streitend und des sieges
Noch ungewiss, lieh neue kraft dies flüstern:
RETURNENT FRANC EN FRANCE DULCE TERRE.

1907

FRANKISH LANDS: Stefan George

Most evil was this forking of my ways:
There, from the chasm, tongues of baneful fire,
Here, regions to be shunned where loathing festered
In me for everything they praised and practised.
I scoffed at their gods, mine they taunted! Where is
Your poet, poor and boastful people? None
Is here: for This One spends his days in exile,
And That One's frantic head is veiled in frost.

The West then called with fabled voice . . . so rang
The sire's praise of his forever lavish
Young land, whose glory thrilled, whose travail moved him
To tears, though he was distant, of the Mother
Of aliens, of the unesteemed and banished . . .
The heir was greeted by a surge when luring
In kindliness and plenitude, the basins
Of Meuse and Marne were spread beneath the sunrise.

And in the town of merry grace, in gardens
Of wistful charm, near nightly gleaming towers
With magic arches, youth was all about me
And swept away with all the things I cherish—
There bard and hero fended for the Secret:
VILLIERS who thought himself the peer of kings,
VERLAINE in fall and shrift devout and childlike,
And bleeding for his concept, MALLARMÉ.

Though dream and distance give us strength and nurture—
Air that we breathe, the Living only proffer.
So friends who still are singing there, I thank you
And forbears that to graves I since have followed . . .
When I had gained a foothold—late—how often
As in my dreary land I strove, uncertain
Of victory, this whisper gave new vigours:
RETURNENT FRANC EN FRANCE DULCE TERRE.

Translated by
Carol North Valhope and Ernst Morwitz

1907

35

Wer, wenn ich schriee, hörte mich denn aus der Engel
Ordnungen? und gesetzt selbst, es nähme
einer mich plötzlich ans Herz: ich verginge von seinem
stärkeren Dasein. Denn das Schöne ist nichts
als des Schrecklichen Anfang, den wir noch grade ertragen,
und wir bewundern es so, weil es gelassen verschmäht,
uns zu zerstören. Ein jeder Engel ist schrecklich.
Und so verhalt ich mich denn und verschlucke den Lockruf
dunkelen Schluchzens. Ach, wen vermögen
wir denn zu brauchen? Engel nicht, Menschen nicht,
und die findigen Tiere merken es schon,
daß wir nicht sehr verläßlich zu Haus sind
in der gedeuteten Welt. Es bleibt uns vielleicht
irgendein Baum an dem Abhang, daß wir ihn täglich
wiedersähen; es bleibt uns die Straße von gestern
und das verzogene Treusein einer Gewohnheit,
der es bei uns gefiel, und so blieb sie und ging nicht.
O und die Nacht, die Nacht, wenn der Wind voller Weltraum
uns am Angesicht zehrt—, wem bliebe sie nicht, die ersehnte,
sanft enttäuschende, welche dem einzelnen Herzen
mühsam bevorsteht. Ist sie den Liebenden leichter?
Ach, sie verdecken sich nur miteinander ihr Los.
Weißt du's noch nicht? Wirf aus den Armen die Leere
zu den Räumen hinzu, die wir atmen; vielleicht daß die Vögel
die erweiterte Luft fühlen mit innigerm Flug.

Ja, die Frühlinge brauchten dich wohl. Es muteten manche
Sterne dir zu, daß du sie spürtest. Es hob
sich eine Woge heran im Vergangenen, oder
da du vorüberkamst am geöffneten Fenster,
gab eine Geige sich hin. Das alles war Auftrag.
Aber bewältigtest du's? Warst du nicht immer
noch von Erwartung zerstreut, als kündigte alles
eine Geliebte dir an? (Wo willst du sie bergen,
da doch die großen fremden Gedanken bei dir

THE FIRST ELEGY: Rainer Maria Rilke

Who, if I cried, would hear me among the angelic
orders? And even if one of them suddenly
pressed me against his heart, I should fade in the strength of his
stronger existence. For Beauty's nothing
but beginning of Terror we're still just able to bear,
and why we adore it so is because it serenely
disdains to destroy us. Each single angel is terrible.
And so I repress myself, and swallow the call-note
of depth-dark sobbing. Alas, who is there
we can make use of? Not angels, not men;
and already the knowing brutes are aware
that we don't feel very securely at home
within our interpreted world. There remains, perhaps,
some tree on a slope, to be looked at day after day,
there remains for us yesterday's walk and the pampered loyalty
of a habit that liked us and stayed and never gave notice.
Oh, and there's Night, there's Night, when wind full of cosmic
    space
feeds on our faces: for whom would she not remain,
longed for, mild disenchantress, painfully there
for the lonely heart to achieve? Is she lighter for lovers?
Alas, with each other they only conceal their lot!
Don't you know *yet*?—Fling the emptiness out of your arms
into the spaces we breathe—maybe that the birds
will feel the extended air in more fervent flight.

Yes, the Springs had need of you. Many a star
was waiting for you to espy it. Many a wave
would rise in the past towards you; or else, perhaps,
as you went by an open window, a violin
would be giving itself to someone. All this was a trust.
But were you equal to it? Were you not always
distracted by expectation, as though all this
were announcing someone to love? (As if you could hope
to house her, with all those great strange thoughts

aus und ein gehn und öfters bleiben bei Nacht.)
Sehnt es dich aber, so singe die Liebenden; lange
noch nicht unsterblich genug ist ihr berühmtes Gefühl.
Jene, du neidest sie fast, Verlassenen, die du
so viel liebender fandst als die Gestillten. Beginn
immer von neuem die nie zu erreichende Preisung;
denk: es erhält sich der Held, selbst der Untergang war ihm
nur ein Vorwand, zu sein: seine letzte Geburt.
Aber die Liebenden nimmt die erschöpfte Natur
in sich zurück, als wären nicht zweimal die Kräfte,
dieses zu leisten. Hast du der Gaspara Stampa
denn genügend gedacht, daß irgendein Mädchen,
dem der Geliebte entging, am gesteigerten Beispiel
dieser Liebenden fühlt: daß ich würde wie sie?
Sollen nicht endlich uns diese ältesten Schmerzen
fruchtbarer werden? Ist es nicht Zeit, daß wir liebend
uns vom Geliebten befrein und es bebend bestehn:
wie der Pfeil die Sehne besteht, um gesammelt im
     Absprung
mehr zu sein als er selbst. Denn Bleiben ist nirgends.

Stimmen, Stimmen. Höre, mein Herz, wie sonst nur
Heilige hörten: daß sie der riesige Ruf
aufhob vom Boden; sie aber knieten,
Unmögliche, weiter und achtetens nicht:
So waren sie hörend. Nicht daß du Gottes ertrügest
die Stimme, bei weitem. Aber das Wehende höre,
die ununterbrochene Nachricht, die aus Stille sich
     bildet.
Es rauscht jetzt von jenen jungen Toten zu dir.
Wo immer du eintratst, redete nicht in Kirchen
zu Rom und Neapel ruhig ihr Schicksal dich an?
Oder es trug eine Inschrift sich erhaben dir auf,
wie neulich die Tafel in Santa Maria Formosa.
Was sie mir wollen? leise soll ich des Unrechts

going in and out and often staying overnight!)
No, when longing comes over you, sing the great lovers:
   the fame
of all they can feel is far from immortal enough.
Those whom you almost envy, those forsaken, you found
so far beyond the requited in loving. Begin
ever anew their never-attainable praise.
Consider: the Hero continues, even his setting
was a pretext for further existence, an ultimate birth.
But lovers are taken back by exhausted Nature
into herself, as though such creative force
could not be exerted twice. Does Gaspara Stampa
mean enough to you yet, and that any girl, whose beloved
has slipped away, might feel, from that far intenser
example of loving: "Could I but become like her!"?
Ought not these oldest sufferings of ours to be yielding
more fruit by now? Is it not time that, in loving,
we freed ourselves from the loved one, and, quivering, endured:
as the arrow endures the string, to become, in the gathering
   out-leap,
something more than itself? For staying is nowhere.

Voices, voices. Hearken, my heart, as only
saints have done: till it seemed the gigantic call
must lift them aloft; yet they went impossibly
on with their kneeling, in undistracted attention:
so inherently hearers. Not that you could endure
the voice of God—far from it. But hark to the suspiration,
the uninterrupted news that grows out of silence.
Rustling towards you now from those youthfully-dead.
Whenever you entered a church in Rome or in Naples
were you not always being quietly addressed by their fate?
Or else an inscription sublimely imposed itself on you,
as, lately, the tablet in Santa Maria Formosa.
What they require of me? I must gently remove the appearance

Anschein abtun, der ihrer Geister
reine Bewegung manchmal ein wenig behindert.

Freilich ist es seltsam, die Erde nicht mehr zu bewohnen,
kaum erlernte Gebräuche nicht mehr zu üben,
Rosen, und andern eigens versprechenden Dingen
nicht die Bedeutung menschlicher Zukunft zu geben;
das, was man war in unendlich ängstlichen Händen,
nicht mehr zu sein, und selbst den eigenen Namen
wegzulassen wie ein zerbrochenes Spielzeug.
Seltsam, die Wünsche nicht weiterzuwünschen. Seltsam,
alles, was sich bezog, so lose im Raume
flattern zu sehen. Und das Totsein ist mühsam
und voller Nachholn, daß man allmählich ein wenig
Ewigkeit spürt.—Aber Lebendige machen
alle den Fehler, daß sie zu stark unterscheiden.
Engel (sagt man) wüßten oft nicht, ob sie unter
Lebenden gehn oder Toten. Die ewige Strömung
reißt durch beide Bereiche alle Alter
immer mit sich und übertönt sie in beiden.

Schließlich brauchen sie uns nicht mehr, die Früheentrückten,
man entwöhnt sich des Irdischen sanft, wie man den Brüsten
milde der Mutter entwächst. Aber wir, die so große
Geheimnisse brauchen, denen aus Trauer so oft
seliger Fortschritt entspringt—: könnten wir sein ohne sie?
Ist die Sage umsonst, daß einst in der Klage um Linos
wagende erste Musik dürre Erstarrung durchdrang,
daß erst im erschrockenen Raum, dem ein beinah göttlicher
    Jüngling
plötzlich für immer enttrat, das Leere in jene
Schwingung geriet, die uns jetzt hinreißt und tröstet und hilft.

Januar 1912

of suffered injustice, that hinders
a little, at times, their purely-proceeding spirits.

True, it is strange to inhabit the earth no longer,
to use no longer customs scarcely acquired,
not to interpret roses, and other things
that promise so much, in terms of a human future;
to be no longer all that one used to be
in endlessly anxious hands, and to lay aside
even one's proper name like a broken toy.
Strange, not to go on wishing one's wishes. Strange,
to see all that was once relation so loosely fluttering
hither and thither in space. And it's hard, being dead,
and full of retrieving before one begins to espy
a trace of eternity.—Yes, but all of the living
make the mistake of drawing too sharp distinctions.
Angels (they say) are often unable to tell
whether they move among living or dead. The eternal
torrent whirls all the ages through either realm
for ever, and sounds above their voices in both.

They've finally no more need of us, the early-departed,
one's gently weaned from terrestrial things as one mildly
outgrows the breasts of a mother. But we, that have need of
such mighty secrets, we, for whom sorrow's often
source of blessedest progress, could we exist without them?
Is the story in vain, how once, in the mourning for Linos,
venturing earliest music pierced barren numbness, and how,
in the startled space an almost deified youth
suddenly quitted for ever, emptiness first
felt the vibration that now charms us and comforts and helps?

Translated by
January 1912   *J. B. Leishman and Stephen Spender*

2. Modernism and the Fusion of the Arts

The series of explosions which took place in painting from 1905 (the birth of the Fauves) onwards inevitably reacted upon poetry. From about 1870, poetry had held the initiative. Even making the fullest allowances for the originality of the Impressionists, the most radical experiments were being made with words. But now, at least to some extent, poetry began to follow in the footsteps of painting.

On the whole, if one examines what was produced in the eleven vital years from 1911 to 1922, it is impossible to separate the contribution of the painters from that of the poets. They lived together and worked together. Apollinaire was the apologist for the Cubists, Marinetti was the founder of Italian Futurism. Many men, such as Hans Arp among the Dadaists, were equally important as poets and painters. To illustrate this section I have brought together a small group of poems which show poetry deliberately imitating painting, and influenced by its procedures.

The first poem in this section, 'The Warmth', is by the minor Russian writer Benedict Konstantinovich Livshits and was written in 1911. Livshits, partly influenced by Mallarmé's ellipses of meaning, is here trying to apply the principles of *avant-garde* painting to words. The technique is one of 'removal', and seems to be related to Kandinsky's essay in the catalogue of an exhibition called *Salon 2*, which was shown in Odessa, Kiev and St Petersburg in 1910–11. Kandinsky remarks, for instance, that: 'A work of art is an indissolubly, necessarily and inevitably linked combination of inner and outer elements, i.e., of content and form. . . .'

The poem is set in a warmly lighted room, where a child, falling asleep, watches a housekeeper rummage in an old wooden chest of drawers. Outside is a snowy landscape. Among the equivalents (the transmutations take place in the child's mind) are the following. The chest, with 'nut-brown belly', is a dead negro. The whiteness of the falling snow contains the seven colours of the spectrum, hence 'peacock tail'. The 'night of mounds' is a reference to the tumuli of South Russia—burial places of dead warriors which look like skulls. It is from the South Russian steppes that the blizzard comes sweeping in.

The next poem is from *Dix-Neuf poèmes elastiques* by Blaise Cendrars. Cendrars' importance as an innovator is still too little recognized outside France. He anticipated many of Apollinaire's experiments, and quite certainly influenced the latter. 'Dernière Heure' is a 'found poem', taken from a newspaper cutting, which precedes many other experiments of this sort. The real reason for placing it in this section is that it provides an equivalent for the experiments with collage which Braque and Picasso were making at the same period—often, as it happens, with cuttings from newspapers. Precisely the same sort of questioning of reality is implied.

There follows a poem by Pierre Reverdy, 'L'Ombre du mur' from his early collection *Les Ardoises du toit* (1918). Reverdy was also connected with the Cubist circle, and the curious overlapping, backward-and-forward movement of the syntax of the poem is an equivalent for the way in which objects are constructed in Cubist pictures, in overlapping planes.

'Natures mortes' by Cendrars, again from *Dix-Neuf poèmes elastiques*, is included as a parallel for the better-known poem by Apollinaire which follows it. 'Les Fenêtres' was first published in January 1913 with a dedication to the painter Robert Delaunay. It is intended as a poetic tribute to a series of pictures called *Windows* which Delaunay had painted towards the end of 1912. The poem, however, seems to use images drawn not from these highly abstract compositions (they are among the earliest truly abstract pictures) but from the work which Delaunay had been doing immediately before. The most striking comparison is with Delaunay's *La Ville de Paris* of 1910–11, of which Apollinaire said that it 'appears to be a synthesis of the whole modern world'. The poem suggests a number of other comparisons also: the dislocated picture of urbanism casts back to Rimbaud's 'Villes II'; the scraps of conversation which turn up in the texture of the verse owe something to Laforgue but more to Cubist *collages*.

The final poem in the section, 'Il Pleut', is one of Apollinaire's celebrated Calligrammes, which are among the few experimental poems known to most people. Apollinaire's aim was to break free altogether of the tyranny of conventional formats—to make the shape of the poem mime the content. In making his way towards this position he had been influenced by Marinetti's *parole in libertà* (for a discussion of which see Section IV), and not the other way round, as is sometimes stated.

The Calligrammes stand at the beginning of a long series of experiments which were to result in the 'concrete poetry' written in many languages in the years immediately following the Second World War. The synthesis is not yet complete, however. Words and pictorial form still exist to some extent independently of one another.

Вскрывай ореховый живот,
Медлительный палач бушмена:
До смерти не растает пена
Твоих старушечьих забот.

Из вечно-желтой стороны
Еще не додано объятий—
Благослови пяту дитяти,
Как парус, падающий в сны.

И, мирно простираясь ниц,
Не знай, что за листами канув,
Павлиний хвост в ночи курганов
Сверлит отверстия глазниц.

1911

O, open up his nut-brown belly,
Slow killer of the bush-man, you.
Till death comes nothing will undo
The foam of your old-woman's worry.

And from the side with yellow streaming,
More huggings must be given yet—
So bless the foot of this child-pet,
Who like a sail sinks into dreaming.

And, calmly, prostrate, try ignoring
The peacock tail (past trees' background)
Falling into the night of mounds,
Into the deep eye-sockets boring.

Translated by
1911   *Vladimir Markov and Merrill Sparks*

OKLAHOMA, *20 janvier 1914*
Trois forçats se procurent des revolvers
Ils tuent leur geôlier et s'emparent des clefs de la prison
Ils se précipitent hors de leurs cellules et tuent quatre gardiens
dans la cour
Puis ils s'emparent de la jeune sténo-dactylographe de la prison
Et montent dans une voiture qui les attendait à la porte
Ils partent à toute vitesse
Pendant que les gardiens déchargent leurs revolvers dans la
direction des fugitifs

Quelques gardiens sautent à cheval et se lancent à la poursuite
des forçats
Des deux côtés des coups de feu sont échangés
La jeune fille est blessée d'un coup de feu tiré par un des
gardiens

Une balle frappe à mort le cheval qui emportait la voiture
Les gardiens peuvent approcher
Ils trouvent les forçats morts le corps criblé de balles
Mr Thomas, ancien membre du Congrès qui visitait la prison
Félicite la jeune fille

Télégramme-poème copié dans *Paris-Midi*

Janvier 1914

STOP PRESS: Blaise Cendrars

OKLAHOMA, *20th January, 1914*
Three convicts possessed themselves of revolvers
Killed their warder and seized the keys of the prison
Burst out of their cells and killed four guards in the courtyard
Then they seized the prison's young stenographer
And getting into a vehicle which was waiting at the gate
Departed at high speed
While the guards fired their revolvers at the fugitives

Some guards leaped on horseback and went in pursuit of the
    fugitives
Shots were exchanged on both sides
The girl was wounded by a shot from one of the guards

A bullet killed the horse which was drawing the vehicle
The guards were able to come up
They found the convicts dead their bodies riddled with bullets
Mr Thomas former Congressman who was visiting the prison
Congratulated the girl

Telegram-poem taken from *Paris-Midi*

January 1914

*Translated by
Edward Lucie-Smith*

Un œil crevé par une plume
Larme qui tombe de la lune
     Un lac
Le monde rentre dans un sac
     La nuit
Les cyprès font le même signe
En blanc la route les souligne
Le paysage hivernal est bleu
        Les doigts tremblent
Deux grands carrés qui se ressemblent
Les ombres dansent au milieu
Des bêtes qu'on ne voit pas
     Des voix

Tout le long du chemin
       Il pleut

c. 1918

THE SHADOW OF THE WALL: Pierre Reverdy

An eye burst by a pen
Tear falling from the moon
        A lake
The world goes back into a bag
          At night
The cypresses make the same sign
The road beneath them a white line
The winter landscape is blue
           The fingers shake
Two great squares alike
The shadows dance amid
Animal noises
        Voices

All along the road
        Rain

c. 1918

Translated by
Keith Bosley

pour Roger de la Fresnaye

Vert
Le gros trot des artilleurs passe sur la géométrie
Je me dépouille
Je ne serais bientôt qu'en acier
Sans l'équerre de la lumière
Jaune
Clairon de modernité
Le classeur américain
Est aussi sec et
Frais
Que vertes les campagnes premières
Normandie
Et la table de l'architecte
Est ainsi strictement belle
Noir
Avec une bouteille d'encre de Chine
Et des chemises bleues
Bleu
Rouge
Puis il y a aussi un litre, un litre de sensualité
Et cette haute nouveauté
Blanc
Des feuilles de papier blanc

Avril 1914

for Roger de la Fresnaye

Green
The heavy trot of the artillerymen goes by on the geometry
I strip myself down
Soon I shall be steel only
Lacking the set-square of the light
Yellow
Clarion of modernity
The American filing-cabinet
Is as spare and
Fresh
As the virgin lands are green
Normandy
And the architect's table
Is likewise strictly beautiful
Black
With a bottle of Chinese ink
And blue shirts
Blue
Red
Then there's also a quart, a quart of sensuality
And this superb novelty
White
Sheets of white paper

April 1914

Translated by
Edward Lucie-Smith

Du rouge au vert tout le jaune se meurt
Quand chantent les aras dans les forêts natales
Abatis de pihis
Il y a un poème à faire sur l'oiseau qui n'a qu'une aile
Nous l'enverrons en message téléphonique
Traumatisme géant
Il fait couler les yeux
Voilà une jolie jeune fille parmi les jeunes Turinaises
Le pauvre jeune homme se mouchait dans sa cravate
  blanche
Tu soulèveras le rideau
Et maintenant voilà que s'ouvre la fenêtre
Araignées quand les mains tissaient la lumière
Beauté pâleur insondables violets
Nous tenterons en vain de prendre du repos
On commencera à minuit
Quand on a le temps on a la liberté
Bigorneaux Lotte multiples Soleils et l'Oursin du couchant
Une vieille paire de chaussures jaunes devant la fenêtre
Tours
Les Tours ce sont les rues
Puits
Puits ce sont les places
Puits
Arbres creux qui abritent les Câpresses vagabondes
Les Chabins chantent des airs à mourir
Aux Chabines marronnes
Et l'oie oua-oua trompette au nord
Où les chasseurs de ratons
Raclent les pelleteries
Étincelant diamant
Vancouver
Où le train blanc de neige et de feux nocturnes fuit l'hiver
O Paris

WINDOWS: Guillaume Apollinaire

The yellow fades from red to green
When aras sing in their native forest
Pihis giblets
There is a poem to be done on the bird with only one wing
We'll send it by telephone
Giant traumatism
It makes one's eyes run
There is one pretty one among all the young girls from Turin
The unfortunate young man blows his nose in his white necktie
You will lift the curtain
And now look at the window opening
Spiders when hands were weaving light
Beauty paleness unfathomable violet tints
We shall try in vain to take our ease
They start at midnight
When one has time one has liberty
Periwinkles turbot multiple Suns and the Sea-urchin of the
    setting sun
An old pair of yellow shoes in front of the window
Towers
Towers are streets
Wells
Wells are market places
Wells
Hollow trees which shelter vagabond Capresses
The Octoroons sing songs of dying
To their chestnut-coloured wives
And the goose honk honk trumpets in the north
When racoon hunters
Scrape their pelts
Gleaming diamond
Vancouver
Where the train white with snow and fires of the night flees
    the winter
O Paris

Du rouge au vert tout le jaune se meurt
Paris Vancouver Hyères Maintenon New-York et les Antilles
La fenêtre s'ouvre comme une orange
Le beau fruit de la lumière

Janvier 1913

The yellow fades from red to green
Paris Vancouver Hyères Maintenon New York and the Antilles
The window opens like an orange
Lovely fruit of light

January 1913

Translated by
Roger Shattuck

IL PLEUT: Guillaume Apollinaire

il pleut des voix de femmes comme si elles étaient mortes même dans le souvenir

c'est vous aussi qu'il pleut merveilleuses rencontres de ma vie ô gouttelettes

et ces nuages cabrés se prennent a hennir tout un univers de villes auriculaires

écoute s'il pleut tandis que le regret et le dédain pleurent une ancienne musique

écoute tomber les liens qui te retiennent en haut et en bas

1918

IT'S RAINING: Guillaume Apollinaire

its raining womens voices as if they were dead even to memory

its you too that its raining marvellous encounters of my life o droplets

and these rearing clouds go whinnying by a whole universe of auricular towns

listen if its raining while regret and disdain weep an ancient music

hear the bonds fall which hold you above and below

Translated by
Edward Lucie-Smith

1918

59

3. The Language Laboratory

That modernist poets would imitate the example of modernist painters in trying to break the moulds of the past was almost inevitable. Poetry followed, though with less determination and upon a smaller scale, the course of development which led to the rise of a wholly abstract art. But there were also those who contributed to this tradition of experiment without perhaps intending to do so. Conspicuous among them was the German poet Christian Morgenstern whose burlesque poems anticipate Dada. The 'Fisches Nachtgesang' is, however, something different, even for Morgenstern: perhaps the earliest attempt to create something which would be recognizable as a poem without using words at all. It has been described as 'the only wholly translatable poem' as a result.

The other poems in this section are largely experiments with sound. Gertrude Stein has usually been discounted as a poet. 'Bee Time Vine' belongs to her most boldly experimental epoch, and dates from 1913, though it remained unpublished until recently. The composer Virgil Thomson, who edited the posthumous volume of uncollected writings in which it appeared, remarks that 'as in *Tender Buttons*, the aim is "to describe a thing without mentioning it". The subject is Spain, probably Granada, and it is a landscape.'

In pieces such as this, Gertrude Stein made what were probably the most extreme experiments which had been undertaken up to that point in English. Few were to go beyond them thereafter, except perhaps James Joyce in *Finnegan's Wake*. Where other languages and cultures were concerned, the situation was different. Russia, before and during the First World War, produced a whole crop of experimental writers. Apart from Mayakovsky, the most important among them was probably Velemir Khlebnikov. Ossip Mandelstam, the greatest of the Acmeists, said that 'Khlebnikov works on words like a mole, and he has bored underground passages into the future for whole centuries ahead'. The poet himself said that he 'wanted

61

to find, without breaking out of the bewitched circle of the roots, the philosopher's stone of the mutual transformation of Slavic words, to fuse freely the Slavic words'. 'Incantation by Laughter', Khlebnikov's best-known experimental poem, which is printed here, consists of newly coined derivations of the word *smekh* (Russian for laughter). Khlebnikov also believed in experimenting in other directions—for instance, by using mathematical symbols and 'syncretic graphic signs' in verse. It is among the Russian Futurists, Khlebnikov and others, that one finds the clearest determination to stress the distinctive function of poetic language, and to differentiate it from all other kinds of communication in speech. Mayakovsky remarked that 'Art is not a copy of nature but the determination to distort nature in accordance with its reflections in the individual consciousness'.

Aleksei Eliseyevich Kruchonykh is a lesser writer than Khlebnikov, but carried his linguistic experiments in some respects even further. Kruchonykh said that he wished to emancipate the word from 'its traditional subservience to meaning', and evolved for this purpose what he described as 'trans-sense language'. He asserted that 'genuine novelty in literature does not depend upon content. . . . A new light thrown on the old world may produce a very interesting interplay.' His application of these principles may be seen in the brief text, 'Heights', printed here which, in its radical simplicity, is reminiscent of Suprematist pictures by Malevich.

Zurich Dada rivalled the Russian and the Italian Futurists in its capacity for uproar. The leading spirit in these early days of the movement was the poet-philosopher Hugo Ball. Before the First World War, Ball was friendly with the painters Kandinsky and Marc, and was interested in the development of abstract painting which Kandinsky was then pioneering. He went to Zurich in 1915, but turned away from Dada as early as 1917. The two sound-poems printed here, 'Totenklage' and 'Seepferdchen und Flugfische', come from a sequence which dates from 1916. Other poets have claimed the credit for inventing the sound-poem. Ball's are certainly both among the earliest, and among the most convincing. They have an eerie likeness to communicative language, without ever quite 'deviating into sense'. They demonstrate, as clearly as any poet has yet managed to do, the possibilities and also the limitations of a wholly abstract literature.

But one must not see Ball as a writer who made a complete break with the past. His titles reveal that he was still concerned, just as Laforgue had been, with communicating a mood, if not specific information. A study of the poems in Laforgue's *Derniers Vers* reveals them to be already very dependent on a linked chain of sound effects, almost independent of meaning. The development from Symbolism to Ball's experiments is a continuous and logical one.

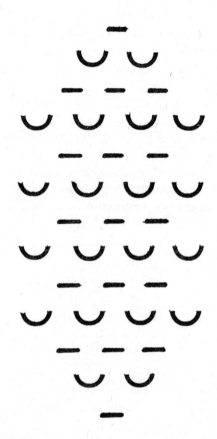

* Fish's Nightsong

Bee time vine be vine truth devine truth.

Be vine be vine be vine truth, be vine be vine be vine.

Class grass not so mange not a linen starch not emblem. Not in blend blemish and a tooth. Love callous kidding with little lozenges and a mouth and moist neglected pens pens full of under standing bold ess with leases and below, below whites, glaze and exchange water with sooth for soot and lower for a cat which is a goat. It was so fine.

Response. Responder to a sofa with and measles four and coolidge paint and neathless which never bless and more colloose with it. Please bet.

Go gout.

A cook makes cake and never less never less grating which be when. This noon.

A lass which moists the beat wax so and it was a ring it was a necessary trim. Alright.

No taste in two.

No twine in two and a best set.

Coal hole.

If coal oil means water and a memory and fine.

Which pen.

Leaves in, no boat.

This is a talk.

Plain grease in covers.

Covers, covers, little lamb.

No poe, coop ham.

Leaf as not.

Ixtact, lime.

Co hie.

Wee nus, poodle nut, all bow with cut hup. Leave len. A go lash. Lips tip. No pie. Rest.

We tight, Nigger. Nasal, noseite. Not we when. Butt, but set. All that, cold. nigh jigger.

Pea sells. All.

Way mouth, soph, chive, bee, so, it, any, muse, in, lee, vie.

1913

C

О, рассмейтесь, смехачи!
О, засмейтесь, смехачи!
Что смеются смехами, что смеянствуют смеяльно.
О, засмейтесь усмеяльно!
О, рассмешищ надсмеяльных—смех усмейных
смехачей!
О, иссмейся рассмеяльно, смех надсмейных смеячей!
Смейево, смейево,
Усмей, осмей, смешики, смешики,
Смеюнчики, смеюнчики,
О, рассмейтесь, смехачи!
О, засмейтесь, смехачи!

1910

INCANTATION BY LAUGHTER: Velemir Khlebnikov

O you laughniks, laugh it out!
O you laughniks, laugh it forth!
You who laugh it up and down, laugh along so laughily;
Laugh it off belaughingly!
Laughters of the laughing laughniks, overlaugh the laughathons!
Laughiness of the laughish laughers, counterlaugh the
Laughdom's laughs!
Laughio! Laughio!
Dislaugh, relaugh, laughlets, laughlets,
Laughulets, laughulets.
O you laughniks, laugh it out!
O you laughniks, laugh it forth!

1910   *Translated by*
Vladimir Markov and Merrill Sparks

ВЫСОТЫ (вселенский язык): Aleksei Eliseyevich Kruchonykh

```
      е у ю
      и а о
       о а
  о а е е и е я
       о а
     е у и е и
      и е е
и и ы и е и и ы
```

1913

HEIGHTS (Universal Language): Aleksei Eliseyevich Kruchonykh

e u w
i a o
o a
o a e e i e w
o a
e u i e i
i e e
i i y i e i i y

1913

Translated by
Vladimir Markov and Merrill Sparks

TOTENKLAGE*: Hugo Ball

ombula
take
bitdli
solunkola
tabla tokta tokta takabla
taka tak
Babula m'balam
tak tru–ü
wo–um
biba bimbel
o kla o auw
kia o auwa
la–auma
o kla o ü
la o auma
klinga–o–e–auwa
ome o–auwa
klinga inga M ao–Auwa
omba dij omuff pomo–auwa
tru–ü
trou–u–ü o–a–o–ü
mo–auwa
gomun guma zangaga gago blagaga
szagaglugi m ba–o–auma
szaga szago
szaga la m'blama
bschigi bschigo
bschigi bschigi
bschiggo bschiggo
goggo goggo
ogoggo
a–o–auma
1916

* Lament for the Dead

70

SEEPFERDCHEN UND FLUGFISCHE*: Hugo Ball

tressli bessli nebogen leila
flusch kata
ballubasch
zack hitti zopp

zack hitti zopp
hitti betzli betzli
prusch kata
ballubasch
fasch kitti bimm

zitti kitillabi billabi billabi
zikko di zakkobam
fisch kitti bisch

bumbalo bumbalo bumbalo bambo
zitti kitillabi
zack hitti zopp

treßli beßli nebogen grügü
blaulala violabimini bisch
violabimini bimini bimini
fusch kata
ballubasch
zick hiti zopp
1916

* Sea-horses and Flying Fish

4. War

The major political event of the period under discussion was, of course, the First World War. It often seems that the violence of the modernist revolution foreshadowed the physical violence of the battlefields: the unleashing of creative energies was immediately followed by the unleashing of the energies of destruction. Many of the leading modernists were apostles of violence—most of the Russian *avant-garde* were enthusiastically on the side of the Revolution, for example. But the noisiest and the most persistent advocates of violence in all its forms were the Italian Futurists, under the leadership of Filippo Tommaso Marinetti. Marinetti is perhaps best described as a charlatan of genius. His proclamations and manifestoes are a strange mixture of nonsense and prescience. Crude nationalism and the shrillest possible self-advertisement mingle with brilliant insights into the future. Marinetti was an enthusiast for war. He even went so far as to head one of the sections of his book, *Le Futurisme*, published in 1911, 'La guerre, seule hygiène du monde'. Nor was he wholly without experience of what war was like. He went to the front when Italy was at war with the Turks in Tripoli, and attended the Siege of Adrianople in 1912, during the Balkan Wars. The fragment entitled 'Bombardamento di Adrianopoli', printed here, is an extract chosen by Marinetti himself, for one of his anthologies of Futurist verse, from his longer work, *Zang-tumb Tum*. This was the most ambitious specimen of what Marinetti called *parole in libertà*—experiments meant to bring to literature the characteristics of Futurist painting, with its emphasis on simultaneity. Marinetti's poetry, either in French or in Italian (he was bilingual), has not won much praise from literary critics, though his recitations of Futurist texts caused a sensation at the time. They are, nevertheless, important 'laboratory experiments', whose influence can be traced in much verse written subsequently—for example, in the 'projective verse' of the Black Mountain School of poets in post-war America.

Max Jacob's prose-poem, 'La Guerre', was also written before the outbreak of hostilities. In a prefatory note to his book *Le Cornet à dès*, published in 1916, Jacob claims that the poems which seem to allude to the War were written as early as 1909, and 'can be called prophetic'. He adds 'they date from a time when we did not know about collective suffering. I foresaw the facts, but had no presentiment of the horror.' Nevertheless, 'La Guerre' and other texts on the same theme, give an interesting example of the way in which the political climate of the times had already set sensitive nerves a-jangling—even the nerves of a man who felt, with the Symbolists, that 'a work of art has its own value, and does not derive this from the confrontations which can be made between it and reality'.

The War itself produced a great deal of poetry, as men struggled to set down, to absorb and to deal with, the unexpected and horrifying events wherein they found themselves plunged. The reaction was different in different literatures. English seems to have been the only literature which produced something which could specifically be called 'war poetry'. A number of anthologies of the poetry of the First World War in English have recently appeared, and the subject is again receiving a good deal of attention. It seems curious, however, that the anthologists and critics concerned usually make no reference to poetry describing the War published in other languages.

The usual thesis concerning the English war-poets is that they were not technically experimental because the War itself allowed them no time to develop new techniques: they did what they could with the forms available to them, and these bent and buckled under the strain. This is true of the minor poets of the day, but untrue of some of the greater ones, most notably Wilfred Owen and Isaac Rosenberg, as can be seen from 'Mental Cases' and 'Louse Hunting', the typical examples shown here. These two evolved, under the pressure of war-time experience, towards a highly individual way of writing which is strongly reminiscent of German Expressionist poetry, though the work of the leading Expressionists was probably unfamiliar to both of them. These two, and D. H. Lawrence, were among the most 'advanced' native-born English writers of the period: taken as a whole English poetry looks remarkably stagnant when set beside developments on the Continent. The parallels between Rosenberg's work, and that of the greatest of the German Expressionists, Georg Trakl, are especially close. One often finds them using very similar systems of imagery (compare 'Grodek' and the last stanza of 'Louse Hunting')—an important point, as Expressionist poetry lays such stress on the image, and the relationship of one image to another, as opposed to the other elements in the poem.

Trakl died in the War (in November 1914 after a mental breakdown induced by his war experiences) and so did many of his more gifted German contemporaries. It often seems that their statement was precisely timed from the historical point of view—Expressionist poetry written after the War was coarse compared to that being written as it began. The label 'Expressionist' indicates sufficiently the close link between it and the German painting of the time.

France and Italy also produced some interesting war poetry, as Jean Cocteau's poem, 'La Douche', and 'Veglia' by Giuseppe Ungaretti printed here go to show. As can be seen particularly clearly from the Cocteau poem, war experience forced *avant-garde* writers to reform their techniques. Reality was now so tremendous that there was some point in trying to convey what it was like.

BOMBARDAMENTO DI ADRIANOPOLI (parole in libertà): Filippo Tommaso Marinetti

Ogni 5 secondi cannoni da assedio sventrrrare spazio con un accordo ZZZANG-TUMB TUM ammutinamento di 500 echi per azzannarlo sminuzzarlo sparpagliarlo all'infiniiiito nel centro di quei *zzzang-tumb tumb* spiaccicati (ampiezza 50 kmq.) balzare scoppi tagli pugni batterie tiro rapido violenza ferocia re-go-la-ri-tà questo basso grave scandere gli strani folli agitissimi acuti della battaglia

Furia affanno orecchie occhi narici aperti! attenti! forza! che gioia vedere udire fiutare tutto tutto taratatatatata delle mitragliatrici strillare a perdifiato sotto morsi schiaffi traak-traak frustate pic-pac-pum-tumb pic-pac-pum-tumb pic-pac-pum-tumb bizzarrie salti (200 metri) della fucileria

Giù giù in fondo all'orchestra stagni diguazzare buoi buffali pungoli carri pluff plaff impennarsi di cavalli flic flac zing zing sciaaack illari nitriti iiiiiii ... scapiccii tintinnii 3 battaglioni bulgari in marcia croooc-craaac (lento due tempi) Sciumi Maritza o Karvavena ta ta ta ta ta giii-tumb giii-tumb ZZZANG-TUMB TUMB (280 colpo di partenza) srrrrrrr GRANG-GRANG (colpo in arrivo) croooc-craaac grida degli ufficiali sbatacchiare come piatti d'ottone pan di qua paack di là cing **buuum** cing ciak (presto) ciaciacia-ciaciaak su giù là là intorno in alto attenzione sulla testa ciaack bello! Vampe vampe vampe vampe vampe vampe vampe vampe (ribalta dei forti)

vampe vampe

vampe

vampe   vampe   vampe (ribalta dei forti) laggiù dietro quel fumo Sciukri Pascià comunica telefonicamente con 27 forti in turco in tedesco allò! Ibrahim! Rudolf! allò! allò!

attori ruoli   echi suggeritori   scenari di fumo   fo- reste   applausi

odore di fieno fango sterco non sento più i miei piedi gelati odore di salnitro odore di marcio Timpani flauti

BOMBARDMENT OF ADRIANOPLE: (liberated words): Filippo Tommaso Marinetti

Every 5 seconds siege-cannon riiip with a concerted
ZZZANG-TUMB TUM   silenced by 500 echoes gnashed
smashed scattered to infiiiiinity   in the midst of these
flattened *zzzang-tumb tumbs* (50 sq. km.) leap explosions cuts
blows rapid-fire batteries   violence fierce reg-ul-ar-i-ty
this heavy bass gives rhythm to the strange mad immensely
agitated high voices of the battle
      Fury exhaustion ears eyes nostrils open! watch it! strength!
Marvellous to see hear smell all all taratatatatata of the
machine-guns shrieking at the tops of their voices beneath
bites slaps traak-traak whip-slashes pic-pac-pum-tumb jugglery
clown-leaps (200 metres) of the fusillade
      Down down at the bottom of the orchestra ponds shaken
oxen buffaloes goads waggons pluff plaff horses rearing flic flac
zing zing sciaaak laughter neighing ing-ing-ing uproar
jingling-ing 3 batallions of Bulgarians on the march croook-
craaac (slow double time) Choumi Maritza or Karavena ta ta ta
ta ta whee-tumb whee-tumb ZZZANG-TUMB TUMB (280
fire) srrrrrrr GRANG-GRANG (on target) shouts of officers
clashing together like brass plates pan here pac there ching
booom ching ciak (quick) ciaciacia-ciaciaak above below there
there high up watch your head ciaaak splendid! Flames flames
flames flames flames flames flames flames (footlights for the
forts)
                    flames flames
                                        flames
      flames   flames   flames (footlights for the forts) down
there beyond the river Chukri Pasha telephones orders in
Turkish in German hullo Ibrahim! hullo Rudolph! hullo!
hullo!
actors roles   echoes prompters   decor of smoke
forests   applause
                    smell of hay-mud-shit I can't feel my frozen feet
smell of saltpetre smell of decomposition Drums flutes

77

clarini dovunque basso alto uccelli cinguettare beatitudine
ombrie cip-cip-cip brezza verde mandre don-dan-don-din-bèèè
Orchestra   i pazzi bastonano i professori d'orchestra questi
bastonatissimi suonare suonare Grandi fragori non cancellare
precisare ritagliandoli rumori più piccoli minutissimi rottami
di echi nel teatro ampiezza 300 chilometri quadrati   tumb-
tumb-tumb-tumb-tumb-tumb   Maritza   Tungia sdraiati
fiumi illustri (un ferito lava lava la sua gamba insanguinata
ascoltando fruscii e gluglii di lagrime ricordi verdi ssss gggg)
Monti Ròdopi ritti alture palchi loggione 2000 shrapnels
sbracciarsi esplodere esploodere esplooode esplooodere fazzo-
letti bianchissimi pieni d'oro   tumb-tumb-tumb-tumb 2000
granate protese strappare con schianti schianti schianti schianti
schianti schianti capigliature nerissime tumbtumbtumbtumb-
tumbtumbtumb l'orchestra dei rumori di guerra gonfiarsi
sotto una nota di silenzio tenuta nell'alto cielo pallone sferico
dorato sorvegliare i tiri

1911

BOMBARDMENT OF ADRIANOPLE: (liberated words): Filippo Tommaso Marinetti *(continued)*

clarinets everywhere above below birds twittering happiness
shape cip-cip-cip breezes greenness herds of cattle don-dan-don
din-bèèè Orchestra   madmen striking the professors of the
orchestra these heavily beaten playing playing Huge roarings
no cancellation greater precision redefinition sounds smaller
tiny fragments of echoes in the theatre 300 square kilometres
      tumb-tumb-tumb-tumb-tumb-tumb   Maritza   Tundja
recumbent illustrious rivers (one of the wounded washes
washes his bloody leg hearing rustlings and gurglings of tears
green memories ssss gggg) upright the Rhodope mountains
heights theatre-boxes galleries 2000 shrapnel shells gesticula-
tions exploding explooding explooding white handkerchiefs
full of gold   tumb-tumb-tumb-tumb 2000 grenades artificial
hands tearing out with bursts bursts bursts bursts bursts bursts
the blackest hair tumbtumbtumbtumbtumbtumbtumb the
orchestra of the sounds of war swells under a note of silence
hung high in the sky a golden spherical balloon directing the
fire.

Translated by
Edward Lucie-Smith

1911

79

Les boulevards extérieurs, la nuit, sont pleins de neige; les bandits sont des soldats; on m'attaque avec des rires et des sabres, on me dépouille: je me sauve pour retomber dans un autre carré. Est-ce une cour de caserne, ou celle d'une auberge? que de sabres! que de lanciers! il neige! on me pique avec une seringue: c'est un poison pour me tuer; une tête de squelette voilée de crêpe me mord le doigt. De vagues réverbères jettent sur la neige la lumière de ma mort.

c. 1909

THE WAR: Max Jacob

At night, the avenues at the city's edge are full of snow; the
bandits are soldiers; they attack and plunder me with laughter
and sabres; running away, I tumble into another square on the
board. Is this a barracks' courtyard, or that of an inn? So many
Sabres! And lancers! Snow! Someone pricks me with a syringe:
poison to kill me; a skull veiled in crepe bites my finger. Vague
street-lamps throw upon the snow the light of my death.

c. 1909

Translated by
Edward Lucie-Smith

Who are these? Why sit they here in twilight?
Wherefore rock they, purgatorial shadows,
Drooping tongues from jaws that slob their relish,
Baring teeth that leer like skulls' teeth wicked?
Stroke on stroke of pain,—but what slow panic,
Gouged these chasms round their fretted sockets?
Ever from their hair and through their hands' palms
Misery swelters. Surely we have perished
Sleeping, and walk hell; but who these hellish?

—These are men whose minds the Dead have ravished.
Memory fingers in their hair of murders,
Multitudinous murders they once witnessed.
Wading sloughs of flesh these helpless wander,
Treading blood from lungs that had loved laughter.
Always they must see these things and hear them,
Batter of guns and shatter of flying muscles,
Carnage incomparable, and human squander
Rucked too thick for these men's extrication.

Therefore still their eyeballs shrink tormented
Back into their brains, because on their sense
Sunlight seems a blood-smear; night comes blood-black;
Dawn breaks open like a wound that bleeds afresh.
—Thus their heads wear this hilarious, hideous,
Awful falseness of set-smiling corpses.
—Thus their hands are plucking at each other;
Picking at the rope-knouts of their scourging;
Snatching after us who smote them, brother,
Pawing us who dealt them war and madness.

1918

LOUSE HUNTING: Isaac Rosenberg

Nudes, stark and glistening,
Yelling in lurid glee. Grinning faces
And raging limbs
Whirl over the floor on fire;
For a shirt verminously busy
Yon soldier tore from his throat
With oaths
Godhead might shrink at, but not the lice,
And soon the shirt was aflare
Over the candle he'd lit while we lay.

Then we all sprang up and stript
To hunt the verminous brood.
Soon like a demons' pantomime
This plunge was raging.
See the silhouettes agape,
See the gibbering shadows
Mixed with the baffled arms on the wall.
See Gargantuan hooked fingers
Pluck in supreme flesh
To smutch supreme littleness.
See the merry limbs in that Highland fling
Because some wizard vermin willed
To charm from the quiet this revel
When our ears were half lulled
By the dark music
Blown from Sleep's trumpet.

c. 1917

Am Abend tönen die herbstlichen Wälder
Von tödlichen Waffen, die goldnen Ebenen
Und blauen Seen, darüber die Sonne
Düstrer hinrollt; umfängt die Nacht
Sterbende Krieger, die wilde Klage
Ihrer zerbrochenen Münder.
Doch stille sammelt im Weidengrund
Rotes Gewölk, darin ein zürnender Gott wohnt,
Das vergossne Blut sich, mondne Kühle;
Alle Strassen münden in schwarze Verwesung.
Unter goldnem Gezweig der Nacht und Sternen
Es schwankt der Schwester Schatten durch den schweigenden
    Hain,
Zu grüssen die Geister der Helden, die blutenden Häupter;
Und leise tönen im Rohr die dunklen Flöten des Herbstes.
O stolzere Trauer! ihr ehernen Altäre,
Die heisse Flamme des Geistes nährt heute ein gewaltiger
    Schmerz,
Die ungebornen Enkel.

1914

GRODEK: Georg Trakl

At nightfall the autumn woods cry out
With deadly weapons and the golden plains,
The deep blue lakes, above which more darkly
Rolls the sun; the night embraces
Dying warriors, the wild lament
Of their broken mouths.
But quietly there in the pastureland
Red clouds in which an angry god resides,
The shed blood gathers, lunar coolness.
All the roads lead to blackest carrion.
Under golden twigs of the night and stars
The sister's shade now sways through the silent copse
To greet the ghosts of the heroes, the bleeding heads;
And softly the dark flutes of autumn sound in the reeds.
O prouder grief! You brazen altars,
Today a great pain feeds the hot flame of the spirit,
The grandsons yet unborn.

1914

Translated by
Michael Hamburger

LA DOUCHE: Jean Cocteau

L'usine à faire les morts
Avait son service d'hygiène.
Tous les jours deux cents condamnés,
Vont à la douche.

Deux cents bestiaux tout nus,
Sauf le bracelet matricule.

Ils se débattent presque tous,
Tellement ils ont peur de l'eau.
Ils veulent garder leur chemise.
Mais les fusiliers marins
Savent la valeur de l'eau douce
Qu'on respecte comme une vierge
Sur les voiliers.

On met les capotes, les casques,
A bouillir dans une étuve.
Les casques, on dirait des moules.
La chaleur charme les poux.

Serre chaude. La buée
Cache une drôle de floraison.
Camélias, fumier qu'on force
A fleurir toutes les saisons.

Pauvre chair en fleur, jeunes arbres
Enracinés dans la boue,
Vous attendez, toujours debout
Une promesse de faux marbre.

Tous les rires sont en patois;
Mais, ah! je reconnais un geste ...
Ce voyou se frottant le bras,
Ce cycliste, Paris, c'est toi.

THE SHOWER-BATH: Jean Cocteau

The factory for making dead men
Looked after cleanliness.
Every day two hundred of the condemned
Went to the shower.

Two hundred cattle, naked,
Save for their identity bracelets.

Almost always they tried to get out of it—
They were so much afraid of the water.
They wanted to keep their shirts.
But the marines
Knew the value of fresh water
Respected like a virgin
Aboard ship.

Greatcoats and caps
Were put to boil in a vat,
Caps, like mussel-shells.
The heat drew out the lice.

A hot-house. The steam
Hides a strange sort of flowering.
Camellias, dung-heap compelled
To flower at all seasons.

Pitiful flesh in flower, young trees
Rooted in mud,
Still upright, you await
A sham-marble promise.

All the laughter coarsely accented;
But ah! I recognize this gesture . . .
That tough, rubbing his arm,
That cyclist, is Paris.

Le tour des nègres est un drame.
Ils refusent de se montrer nus.
Ils résistent de toutes leurs forces.
A moitié morts à l'ambulance,
Chargés d'amulettes, d'écorces,
De coquillages inconnus,
De désespoir, de silence,
Ils pensaient à cacher leur sexe.

Les nègres sont Antinoüs
Vu dans un noir miroir convexe.
Malades, ils deviennent mauves.
Ils toussent. Hélas! où sont-elles
Vos îles? et vos crocodiles
Où sont-ils?

Nègres nous avons le cœur dur.
Chez nous on n'aime que l'ennui.
Votre corps, votre âme sont purs,
Comme du corail dans la nuit.

Les zouaves, après la douche,
Se font des farces de collège.
Ils se parlent du bout du monde,
En enroulant leur ceinture.

Maintenant, c'est la chéchia.

Au 4me zouave de marche,
On l'entre sur l'oreille droite.
Elle est basse sur la nuque
Une frange de cheveux dépasse.

Au 3me zouave on la rentre
Par derrière. L'oreille est libre.

When the negroes come, it's a comedy.
They won't be seen naked.
They resist with all their might.
Half-dead in the ambulance,
Hung about with charms, with bark,
With unknown shells,
With despair, with silence,
They still try to hide their private parts.

The negroes are Antinoüs,
Seen in a black convex mirror.
Sick, they go mauve.
They cough. Alas! where are
Your isles, and where
Your crocodiles?

Negroes, we are hard of heart,
We love only boredom.
Your bodies, your souls are pure
Like coral in the night.

The zouaves, after the shower,
Lark about like schoolboys.
They talk about the ends of the earth.
Rolling up their belts.

Now to put on the *chéchia*

With the 4th zouave in the rank
It goes on over his right ear.
It comes low on his neck,
A fringe of hair shows under it.

With the 3rd zouave, it goes
On the back of his head. The ear left free.

Le 2me zouave la porte
Ouverte, le gland en arrière.
Elle cache les oreilles.

Au 1er zouave c'est pareil
Mais sans cacher les oreilles

c. 1917

The 2nd zouave wears it
Open, the tassel behind.
It hides his ears.

The 1st zouave likewise,
But ears uncovered.

c. 1917

Translated by
Edward Lucie-Smith

VEGLIA: Giuseppe Ungaretti

Un'intera nottata
buttato vicino
a un compagno
massacrato
con la sua bocca
digrignata
volta al plenilunio
con la congestione
delle sue mani
penetrata
nel mio silenzio
ho scritto
lettere piene d'amore

Non sono mai stato
tanto
attaccato alla vita

23 Dicembre 1915

WATCH: Giuseppe Ungaretti

One whole night
tossed down beside
a slaughtered
comrade
his snarling
mouth
turned to the full moon
the bloating
of his hands
entering
my silence
I have written
letters full of love

Never have I held
so
fast to life

23 December 1915

Translated by
Allen Mandelbaum

5. Dada

The poetry of the Dadaists has perhaps attracted more attention from art-historians than the rest of the *avant-garde* literature of the time, even the writings of Marinetti and Apollinaire. The reason is that all researchers into Dada have recognized the fact that in this, of all art-movements, poetry and the plastic arts are inseparable. Indeed, they were often produced by the same people. But one can go too far in claiming that Dada poetry is *sui generis*, a phenomenon which it took the War and a certain conjunction of people in neutral Switzerland to produce. Alfred Lichtenstein's 'Der Lackschuh', for instance, dates from 1913—two years before the foundation of Dada, and a year before the outbreak of war. Lichtenstein was killed in September 1914, and can never have heard of Dada or the Dadaists. Yet many of the essential Dada ingredients are already present in his work—the disgust, the irony, the nonsense-element. There is not much difference between Lichtenstein's work and the early poetry of Tristan Tzara, for instance. The Dada style had already been well prepared for in the literature of the time.

There is still some controversy as to what Dada itself really stood for. Was it simply a gesture of disgust at the way things were going in the world? Was it an attempt to overthrow all previous canons in art, and to set up a new 'anti-art' in the place of art itself? Was it an attempt to liberate the mind through the abandonment of logic, the exploitation of dreams, a foreshadowing of Surrealism? The answer seems to be that Dada was all of these things at once.

In a recent account of Dada, the veteran Dadaist Hans Richter remarks that it 'had no unified formal characteristics as have other styles'. This judgment is certainly quite precisely applicable to Dada poetry. The few specimens printed here (by Richard Huelsenbeck, Tristan Tzara, Hans Arp, and Kurt Schwitters—all of them leading figures in the movement) are united only by their determination to be as anti-literary as possible, to flout all accepted norms of poetic organization. This can be seen especially clearly in Kurt Schwitters's own naïve but vigorous translation into English of the best-known text from his book *Anna Blume*.

The notion of the 'anti-literary' has been much slower to establish itself than that of anti-art, and these texts still seem outrageous and extreme in a way which is not true of Dada paintings, collages and sculptures. Arp's reputation as a sculptor is a great deal more secure than his reputation as a poet, though it bears reflection that the sculptures, reliefs and poems are the product of an identical intelligence and an identical sensibility. So are Schwitters's collages and his poems.

It is worth pondering on the reasons why Dada poetry, and indeed experimental poetry in general, has retained its power to shock. The reason seems to be that we regard language as an essentially communicative instrument—perhaps even as an essentially logical and rational instrument. We accept far more easily the idea that a painting or a sculpture may communicate in a pre- or even anti-logical way.

Moholy-Nagy (*Vision in Motion*, p. 314) defends Dada poetry by saying that:

> Traditional poetry displayed the old content. Its form of expression—the one dimensional linear form—was adequate for the ideas formulated. Today a profoundly changed content has to be expressed, precipitated by the industrial revolution with its new social structure and all its ramifications. At present there are no adequate words, symbols, signs—the much-needed structure of communication. One has to be satisfied today with the search.

In fact, the Dadaists did two things. Dissatisfied with the idea of 'literature' as something entirely walled-off, provided with fixed boundaries, and the property of those who had turned themselves into professional 'literary men', they made an extremely effective gesture against the wrong kind of professionalism. Poetry, for them, was something which sprang from a man's very self, the deepest layers of his being, and roughness of form did not matter too much if the expression was honest and authentic. This attitude, in turn, led them towards the Surrealist theory of the primacy of the unconscious mind.

Editor's Note: It might be helpful to the readers to bear in mind that in *End of the World* by Richard Huelsenbeck (pp. 100-103), a more literal rendering of the last line: '(Wer sollte da nicht blödsinnig werden)', might be '(Isn't it enough to drive you barmy?)'.

DER LACKSCHUH: Alfred Lichtenstein

Der Dichter dachte:
Ach was, ich hab den Plunder satt!

Die Dirnen, das Theater und den Stadtmond,
Die Oberhemden, Strassen und Gerüche,
Die Nächte und die Kutscher und die Fenster,
Das Lachen, die Laternen und die Morde—
Den ganzen Dreck hab ich nun wirklich satt,
Beim Teufel!
Mag werden, was da will . . . mir ist es gleich:
Der Lackschuh drückt mich. Und ich zieh ihn aus—

Die Leute mögen sich verwundert wenden.
Nur schade ists um meinen seidnen Strumpf. . . .

1913

THE PATENT LEATHER SHOE: Alfred Lichtenstein

The poet thought:
Enough. I'm sick of the whole lot!

The whores, the theatre and the city moon,
The streets, the laundered shirtfronts and the smells,
The nights, the coachmen and the curtained windows,
The laughter and the streetlamps and the murders—
To hell with it!
Happen what may . . . it's all the same to me:
This black shoe pinches me. I'll take it off—

Let people turn their heads for all I care.
A pity, though, about my new silk sock. . . .

1913

Translated by
Michael Hamburger

ENDE DER WELT: Richard Huelsenbeck

Soweit ist es nun tatsächlich mit dieser Welt gekommen
Auf den Telegraphenstangen sitzen die Kühe und spielen
  Schach
So melancholisch singt der Kakadu unter den Röcken der
spanischen Tänzerin wie ein Stabstrompeter
und die Kanonen jammern
den ganzen Tag
Das ist die Landschaft in Lila von der Herr Mayer sprach als
er das Auge verlor
Nur mit der Feuerwehr ist die Nachtmahr aus dem Salon zu
vertreiben
aber alle Schläuche sind entzwei
Ja ja Sonja da sehen Sie die Zelluloidpuppe als Wechselbalg
an und schreien: God save the king
Der ganze Monistenbund ist auf dem Dampfer 'Meyerbeer'
versammelt
doch nur der Steuermann hat eine Ahnung vom hohen C
Ich ziehe den anatomischen Atlas aus meiner Zehe
ein ernsthaftes Studium beginnt
Habt Ihr die Fische gesehen die im Cutaway vor der Opera
stehen
schon zween Nächte und zween Tage?
Ach Ach Ihr großen Teufel—ach ach Ihr Imker und Platz-
kommandanten
Wille wau wau wau Wille wo wo wo wer weiß heute nicht
was unser Vater Homer gedichtet hat
Ich halte den Krieg und den Frieden in meiner Toga aber ich
entscheide mich für den Cherry-Brandy flip
Heute weiß keiner ob er morgen gewesen ist
Mit dem Sargdeckel schlägt man den Takt dazu
Wenn doch nur einer den Mut hätte der Trambahn die
Schwanzfedern auszureißen es ist eine große Zeit
Die Zoologieprofessoren sammeln sich im Wiesengrund
Sie wehren den Regenbogen mit den Handtellern ab
Der große Magier legt die Tomaten auf seine Stirn

END OF THE WORLD: Richard Huelsenbeck

This is what things have come to in this world
The cows sit on the telegraph poles and play chess
The cockatoo under the skirts of the Spanish dancer
Sings as sadly as a headquarters bugler and the cannon lament
    all day
That is the lavender landscape Herr Mayer was talking about
when he lost his eye
Only the fire department can drive the nightmare from the
drawing-room but all the hoses are broken
Ah yes Sonya they all take the celluloid doll for a changeling
and shout: God save the king
The whole Monist Club is gathered on the steamship Meyerbeer
But only the pilot has any conception of high C
I pull the anatomical atlas out of my toe
a serious study begins
Have you seen the fish that have been standing in front of the
opera in cutaways
for the last two days and nights . . . ?
Ah ah ye great devils—ah ah ye keepers of the bees and
    commandants
With a bow wow wow with a boe woe woe who today does
    not know
what our Father Homer wrote
I hold peace and war in my toga but I'll take a cherry flip
Today nobody knows whether he was tomorrow
They beat time with a coffin lid
If only somebody had the nerve to rip the tail feathers
out of the trolley car it's a great age
The professors of zoology gather in the meadows
With the palms of their hands they turn back the rainbows
the great magician sets the tomatoes on his forehead

Füllest wieder Busch und Schloß
Pfeift der Rehbock hüpft das Roß
(Wer sollte da nicht blödsinnig werden)

1916

Again thou hauntest castle and grounds
The roebuck whistles the stallion bounds
(And this is how the world is this is all that's ahead of us)

1916

Translated by
Ralph Manheim

LA GRANDE COMPLAINTE DE MON OBSCURITÉ TROIS : Tristan Tzara

chez nous les fleurs des pendules s'allument et les plumes
   encerclent la clarté
le matin de soufre lointain les vaches lèchent les lys de sel
mon fils
mon fils

traînons toujours par la couleur du monde
qu'on dirait plus bleue que le métro et que l'astronomie
nous sommes trop maigres
nous n'avons pas de bouche
nos jambes sont raides et s'entrechoquent
nos visages n'ont pas de forme comme les étoiles
cristaux points sans force feu brûlée la basilique
folle : les zigzags craquent
téléphone
mordre les cordages se liquéfier
l'arc
grimper
astrale
la mémoire
vers le nord par son fruit double
comme la chair crue
faim feu sang

1918

GREAT COMPLAINT OF MY OBSCURITY
THREE: Tristan Tzara

with us the flowers of the clocks light up and the feathers
    encircle the brightness
on a morning of distant sulphur the cows lick the lilies of salt
my son
my son

let us crawl forever through the colour of the world
which seems bluer than the metro or astronomy
we are too thin
we have no mouths
our legs are stiff and knock together
our faces are formless like the stars
crystals points without force fire the mad basilica
burnt: the zigzags crackle
telephone
to bite the ropes to melt oneself down
the arch
to climb
astral
memory
northwards through its double fruit
like raw meat
hunger fire blood

1918

Translated by
Edward Lucie-Smith

weh unser guter kaspar ist tot.

wer verbirgt nun die brennende fahne im wolkenzopf und
schlägt täglich ein schwarzes schnippchen.

wer dreht nun die kaffeemühle im urfass.

wer lockt nun das idyllische reh aus der versteinerten tüte.

wer schneuzt nun die schiffe parapluis windeuter bienenväter
ozonspindeln und entgrätet die pyramiden.

weh weh weh unser guter kaspar ist tot. heiliger bimbam
kaspar ist tot.

die heufische klappern herzzerreissend vor leid in den
glockenscheunen wenn man seinen vornamen ausspricht.
darum seufze ich weiter seinen familiennamen kaspar kaspar
kaspar.

warum hast du uns verlassen. in welche gestalt ist nun deine
schöne grosse seele gewandert. bist du ein stern geworden
oder eine kette aus wasser an einem heissen wirbelwind oder
ein euter aus schwarzem licht oder ein durchsichtiger ziegel
an der stöhnenden trommel des felsigen wesens.

jetzt vertrocknen unsere scheitel und sohlen und die feen
liegen halbverkohlt auf dem scheiterhaufen.

jetzt donnert hinter der sonne die schwarze kegelbahn und
keiner zieht mehr die kompasse und die räder der schiebkarren
auf.

wer isst nun mit der phosphoreszierenden ratte am einsamen
barfüssigen tisch.

wer verjagt nun den sirokkoko teufel wenn er die pferde
verführen will.

wer erklärt uns nun die monogramme in den sternen.

seine büste wird die kamine aller wahrhaft edlen menschen
zieren doch ist das kein trost und schnupftabak für einen
totenkopf.

1920

106

KASPAR IS DEAD: Hans Arp

alas our good kaspar is dead.

who'll now hide the burning flag in the cloudpigtail and every day cock a black snook.

who'll now turn the coffeegrinder in the primeval tub.

who'll now lure the idyllic doe from the petrified paperbag.

who'll now blow the noses of ships parapluis windudders beefathers ozonespindles and who'll bone the pyramids.

alas alas alas our good kaspar is dead. saint dingdong kaspar is dead.

the grass-shark rattles his teeth heartrendingly in the bellbarns when his forename is spoken. therefore I shall go on sighing his familyname kaspar kaspar kaspar.

why hast thou forsaken us. into what form has thy great beautiful soul migrated. hast thou become a star or a chain of water hanging from a hot whirlwind or an udder of black light or a transparent tile on the groaning drum of the rocky essence.

now our tops and toes go dry and the fairies are lying halfcharred on the funeral pyre.

now the black skittle alley thunders behind the sun and nobody winds up the compasses and the pushcart wheels any mroe.

who'll now eat with the phosphorescent rat at the lonely barefoot table.

who'll now shoo away the siroccoco devil when he tries to ravish the horses.

who'll now elucidate for us the monograms in the stars.

his bust will grace the mantelpieces of all truly noble men but that's no consolation and snuff for a death's head.

1920

*Translated by
Christopher Middleton*

AN ANNA BLUME: Kurt Schwitters

O du, Geliebte meiner siebenundzwanzig Sinne, ich liebe
dir! — Du deiner dich dir, ich dir, du mir. — Wir?
Das gehört (beiläufig) nicht hierher.
Wer bist du, ungezähltes Frauenzimmer? Du bist — — bist
du? — Die Leute sagen, du wärest, — laß sie sagen, sie
wissen nicht, wie der Kirchturm steht.
Du trägst den Hut auf deinen Füßen und wanderst auf die
Hände, auf den Händen wanderst du.
Hallo, deine roten Kleider, in weiße Falten zersägt.
Rot liebe ich Anna Blume, rot liebe ich dir! — Du deiner
dich dir, ich dir, du mir. — Wir?
Das gehört (beiläufig) in die kalte Glut.
Rote Blume, rote Anna Blume, wie sagen die Leute?
Preisfrage: 1. Anna Blume hat ein Vogel.
            2. Anna Blume ist rot.
            3. Welche Farbe hat der Vogel?
Blau ist die Farbe deines gelben Haares.
Rot ist das Girren deines grünen Vogels.
Du schlichtes Mädchen im Alltagskleid, du liebes grünes Tier,
ich liebe dir! — Du deiner dich dir, ich dir, du mir, — Wir?
Das gehört (beiläufig) in die Glutenkiste.
Anna Blume! Anna; a-n-n-a- ich träufle deinen
Namen. Dein Name tropft wie weiches Rindertalg.
Weißt du es, Anna, weißt du es schon?
Man kann dich auch von hinten lesen, und du, du
Herrlichste von allen, du bist von hinten wie von vorne:
'a-n-n-a'.
Rindertalg träufelt streicheln über meinen Rücken.
Anna Blume, du tropfes Tier, ich liebe dir!
1919

EVE BLOSSOM HAS WHEELS: Kurt Schwitters

O thou, beloved of my twenty-seven senses,
I love thine!
Thou thee thee thine, I thine, thou mine, we?
That (by the way) is beside the point!
Who art thou, uncounted woman,
Thou art, art thou?
People say, thou werst,
Let them say, they don't know what they are talking about.
Thou wearest thine hat on thy feet, and wanderest on thine
    hands,
On thine hands thou wanderest.
Hallo, thy red dress, sawn into white folds,
Red I love eve Blossom, red I love thine!
Thou thee thee thine, I thine, thou mine, we?
That (by the way) belongs to the cold glow!
eve Blossom, red eve Blossom, what do people say?
Prize Question: 1. eve Blossom is red.
                2. eve Blossom has wheels.
                3. what colour are the wheels?
Blue is the colour of your yellow hair,
Red is the whirl of your green wheels,
Thou simple maiden in everyday dress,
Thou small green animal,
I love thine!
Thou thee thee thine, I thine, thou mine, we?
That (by the way) belongs to the glowing brazier!
eve Blossom,
eve,
E-V-E,
E easy, V victory, E easy,
I trickle your name.
Your name drops like soft tallow.
Do you know it, eve,
Do you already know it?
One can also read you from the back.

E

And you, you most glorious of all,
You are from the back as from the front,
E-V-E.
Easy victory.
Tallow trickles to strike over my back!
eve Blossom,
Thou drippy animal,
I
Love
Thine!
I love you! ! !

1919   *Author's translation*

6. The Vision of the Self and the Vision of Reality

The group of poems brought together in this section is not intended to illustrate a specific theme, like those attached to previous sections. Rather, the intention is to show what possibilities were open to modernist poetry after half a century of development.

Spanish poetry had remained somewhat apart, isolated from the other European literatures. The *modernismo* of Rubén Darío, which dominated the early years of the twentieth century, was not at all the same thing as the modernism of Paris, Berlin, Milan or Moscow. But in 1922 there appeared the second book, *Trilce*, of the Peruvian poet César Vallejo. His first collection had appeared four years earlier. *Trilce* is a key work. Vallejo had not yet left Peru for Europe—he was still a provincial. Yet he shows himself to be equipped with a definably 'modern' sensibility. 'Dobla el dos de Noviembre' is more coherent by far than the work of the Dada writers; and yet it is still more concerned to trace the contour of a mind and sensibility than to offer a logical, continuous narrative structure. 'Schwermut', the little poem by August Stramm, printed immediately following it, perhaps offers a hint as to what had happened—it dates from about eight years earlier. Stramm's strange expressive syntax sketches a movement of thought which appears more fully developed, with flesh on its bones, in the poem by Vallejo. Vallejo communicates by juxtaposition of images, by the rhythm in which one image follows another.

The poems by Valéry Larbaud, Gottfried Benn, and Anatoly Borisovich Marienhof which follow are meant to extend and elaborate upon the theme of the poet's relationship to the modern world. 'Madame Tussaud's' comes from Larbaud's volume *Poémes d'un riche amateur*, published in a limited edition in 1908, and reissued with revisions, under the title *Poésies de A. O. Barnabooth*, in 1913. Barnabooth was an imaginary personage—the man of independent means who knows that there is something wrong with the world but who does not know what to do about it—who much resembled Larbaud himself. The real originality of the poems is to be found in their simplicity and matter-of-factness, tinged with irony. Poetry is here being demythologized, and the first stage of the revolt against bourgeois values is visibly consolidating itself.

Benn's poem, 'Nachtcafé', shows a more violent and disgusted reaction—the ugliness described is both an insult to the bourgeoisie and the product of the bourgeoisie itself. Such attitudes were to become the commonplaces of poetic modernism. The difficulty which many poets found in marrying revolutionary sentiments and real poetic experiment is symbolized by Marienhof's little poem. Nearly all bad modernist poetry follows in Marienhof's footsteps, and is characterized by gratuitous shrillness and violence and the desire to shock at almost all costs. The literary standards of the nineteenth century are destroyed, and nothing is put in their place.

The Revolution in Russia did, however, produce at least one great poet, in the person of Vladimir Mayakovsky. Mayakovsky's suicide coincided with the final suppression of modernism in Russia. The extract printed here is taken from his long autobiographical poem, 'The Cloud in Trousers', which dates from 1914–15. One finds here the magnificent, and for all its extravagance, successful assertion of the individuality of the modern writer, of his place in the cosmos. It is, however, important to understand that with Mayakovsky, the wheel has to some extent swung full-circle from the Symbolists. Futurists of Mayakovsky's stamp were filled with scorn for Symbolist talk about inspiration. One critic has remarked that 'Futurism trampled upon the rules of cognitive language not for the sake of a "higher" verbal cognition, but in defence of the free untrammelled verbal play which presumably could dispense with metaphysical sanctions'. Mayakovsky himself called poetry 'a kind of production . . . a very difficult, very complicated one to be sure, but still production'. This brings poetry into line with the developments in the visual arts which were then taking place in Russia: the activity of the Constructivists, for example. The critic Alexei Gan, in his essay-manifesto *Constructivism* (written 1920, published 1922), asserts:

> Intellectual-material production will be expressed in the rising up of a culture of work and the intellect. The first slogan of Constructivism is 'Down with speculative activity in artistic work! We declare unconditional war on art.'

This makes an amusing and instructive comparison with Ezra Pound's 'Salutation the Second', which is my last example. Pound is voicing his realization that the literature of the English-speaking world, or at least the poetry written in English, still had a long way to go before it caught up with developments elsewhere (the poem comes from *Lustra*, which was published in 1915). But even the language in which he makes his statement is inextricably entangled with the past— the archaisms show up glaringly when one compares this text with the simplicity of Larbaud, for instance. The modernism of Eliot and Pound was in many ways a belated offshoot of events which had already taken place in Europe. The fact that modernism found it so difficult to get a foothold in the visual arts in England and America had effects which are still being felt in English and American literature.

Dobla el dos de Noviembre.

Estas sillas son buenas acojidas.
La rama del presentimiento
va, viene, sube, ondea sudorosa,
fatigada en esta sala.
Dobla triste el dos de Noviembre.

Difuntos, qué bajo cortan vuestros dientes
abolidos, repasando ciegos nervios,
sin recordar la dura fibra
que cantores obreros redondos remiendan
con cáñamo inacabable, de innumerables nudos
latientes de encrucijada.

Vosotros, difuntos, de las nítidas rodillas
puras a fuerza de entregaros,
cómo aserráis el otro corazón
con vuestras blancas coronas, ralas
de cordialidad. Sí. Vosotros, difuntos.

Dobla triste el dos de Noviembre.
Y la rama del presentimiento
se la muerde un carro que simplemente
rueda por la calle.

1922

'THE SECOND OF NOVEMBER TOLLS': César Vallejo

The second of November tolls.

These chairs are a place of refuge.
The branch of foreboding
comes and goes, rises, and steaming sways
wearied in this room.
Sadly tolls the second of November.

You dead, how deep your abolished teeth
cut, passing over blind nerves,
forgetful of the tough fibre
that plump singing workers mend
with endless hemp and with innumerable
fluttering crisscross knots.

You, the dead, with bare knees
pure by dint of surrender:
how you hack at the other heart
with your white crowns, sparing
of your cordiality. Yes. You, the dead.

Sadly tolls the second of November.
And the branch of foreboding
is bitten by a simple cart
rolling through the street.

1922

Translated by
Donald D. Walsh

SCHWERMUT: August Stramm

Schreiten Streben
Leben sehnt
Schauern Stehen
Blicke suchen
Sterben wächst
das Kommen
schreit!
Tief
stummen
wir.

dezember, 1914

Striding striving
living longs
shuddering standing
glances look for
dying grows
the coming
screams!
Deeply
we
dumb.

December, 1914

Translated by
Michael Hamburger

Il me semble que toute la sagesse du monde
Est dans les yeux de ces bonshommes en cire.
Je voudrais être enfermé là toute une nuit,
Une nuit d'hiver, par mégarde,
Surtout dans la salle des criminels,
Des bons criminels en cire,
Faces luisantes, yeux ternes, et corps—en quoi?
Mais, est-ce que ça leur ressemble vraiment?
Alors pourquoi les a-t-on enfermés, électrocutés ou pendus,
Pendant que leur image muette reste ici?
Avec des yeux qui ne peuvent pas dire les horreurs souffertes,
Mais qui rencontrent des yeux partout, sans fin, sans fin.
Les ferment-ils au moins la nuit?

1908

MADAME TUSSAUD'S: Valéry Larbaud

It seems to me that all the wisdom of the world
Can be found in the eyes of these wax dummies.
I should like to be shut in there all night long,
One winter night, by inadvertence,
And most of all in the room with the criminals,
Those nice criminals in wax,
Faces shining, eyes lustreless—and bodies made of what?
Do these really look like them?
If so, why have they been shut up, electrocuted or hanged,
While their mute images remain here?
With eyes that cannot tell of the horrors they've undergone,
But which meet other eyes everywhere, endlessly, endlessly.
Do they at least shut them at night?

1908

Translated by
Edward Lucie-Smith

824: Der Frauen Liebe und Leben.
Das Cello trinkt rasch mal. Die Flöte
rülpst tief drei Takte lang: das schöne Abendbrot.
Die Trommel liest den Kriminalroman zu Ende.

Grüne Zähne, Pickel im Gesicht
winkt einer Lidrandentzündung.

Fett im Haar
spricht zu offenem Mund mit Rachenmandel
Glaube Liebe Hoffnung um den Hals.

Junger Kropf ist Sattelnase gut.
Er bezahlt für sie drei Biere.

Bartflechte kauft Nelken,
Doppelkinn zu erweichen.

B-moll: die 35. Sonate.
Zwei Augen brüllen auf:
Spritzt nicht das Blut von Chopin in den Saal,
damit das Pack drauf rumlatscht!
Schluss! He, Gigi!—

Die Tür fliesst hin: ein Weib.
Wüste ausgedörrt. Kanaanitisch braun.
Keusch. Höhlenreich. Ein Duft kommt mit. Kaum Duft.
Es ist nur eine süsse Vorwölbung der Luft
gegen mein Gehirn.

Eine Fettleibigkeit trippelt hinterher.

824: The Love and Life of Women.
The 'cello has a quick drink. The flute
belches throughout three beats: his tasty evening snack.
The drum reads on to the end of the thriller.

Green teeth, pimples on his face,
waves to conjunctivitis.

Grease in his hair
talks to open mouth with swollen tonsils,
faith hope and charity round his neck.

Young goiter is sweet on saddle-nose.
He stands her three half pints.

Sycosis buys carnations
to mollify double chin.

B flat minor: sonata op. 35.
A pair of eyes roars out:
Don't splash the blood of Chopin round the place
for this lot to slouch about in!
Hey, Gigi! Stop!

The door dissolves: a woman.
Desert dried out. Canaanite brown.
Chaste. Full of caves. A scent comes with her. Hardly scent.
It's only a sweet leaning forward of the air
against my brain.

A paunched obesity waddles after her.

Translated by
Michael Hamburger

1917

123

Твердь, твердь за вихры зыбим,
Святость хлещем свистящей нагайкой
И хилое тело Христа на дыбе
Вздыбливаем в Чрезвычайке.

Что же, что же, прощай нам грешным,
Спасай, как на Голгофе разбойника,—
Кровь Твою, кровь бешено
Выплескиваем, как воду из рукомойника.

Кричу: 'Мария, Мария, кого вынашивала!—
Пыль бы ног твоих целовал за аборт! . . .'
Зато теперь: на распеленутой земле нашей
Только Я—человек горд.

1918

We lift the heavens, the heavens by the ears;
We whip holiness to please us.
In Cheka torture-chambers we put on the rack
The sickly body of Jesus.

Well, what of it? Forgive us sinners,
As you did the thief on Golgotha's tree.
As if it were water from a washstand,
We spill your blood furiously.

'Mary, Mary,' I shout, 'See what you bore!
He would kiss your feet gladly if you had aborted Him then!'
But today: in our unswaddled land
Who are the proud ones? Only men!

Translated by
1918   *Vladimir Markov and Merrill Sparks*

Extract from ОБЛАКО В ШТАНАХ:
Vladimir Mayakovsky

Я,
златоустейший,
чье каждое слово
душу новородит,
именинит тело,
говорю вам:
мельчайшая пылинка живого
ценнее всего, что я сделаю и сделал!

Слушайте!
Проповедует,
мечась и стеня,
сегодняшнего дня крикогубый Заратустра!
Мы
с лицом, как заспанная простыня,
с губами, обвисшими, как люстра,
мы,
каторжане города-лепрозория,
где золото и грязь изъязвили проказу,—
мы чище венецианского лазорья,
морями и солнцами омытого сразу!

Плевать, что нет
у Гомеров и Овидиев
людей, как мы,
от копоти в оспе.
Я знаю—
солнце померкло б, увидев
наших душ золотые россыпи!

Жилы и мускулы—молитв верней.
Нам ли вымаливать милостей времени!
Мы—
каждый—

Extract from THE CLOUD IN TROUSERS:
Vladimir Mayakovsky

I,
the most golden-mouthed,
whose every word
gives a new birthday to the soul,
gives a name-day to the body,
I adjure you:
the minutest living speck
is worth more than what I'll do or did!

Listen!
It is today's brazen-lipped Zarathustra
who preaches,
dashing about and groaning!
We,
our face like a crumpled sheet,
our lips pendulant like a chandelier;
we,
the convicts of the City Leprous,
where gold and filth spawned lepers' sores,
we are purer than the azure of Venice,
washed by both the sea and the sun!

I spit on the fact
that neither Homer nor Ovid
invented characters like us,
pock-marked with soot.
I know
the sun would dim, on seeing
the gold fields of our souls!

Sinews and muscles are surer than prayers.
Must we implore the charity of the times!
We—
each one of us—

держим в своей пятерне
миров приводные ремни!

Это взвело на Голгофы аудиторий
Петрограда, Москвы, Одессы, Киева,
и не было ни одного,
который
не кричал бы:
'Распни,
распни его!'
Но мне—
люди,
и те, что обидели—
вы мне всего дороже и ближе.

Видели,
как собака бьющую руку лижет?!

Я,
обсмеянный у сегодняшнего племени,
как длинный
скабрезный анекдот,
вижу идущего через горы времени,
которого не видит никто.

Где глаз людей обрывается куцый,
главой голодных орд,
в терновом венце революций
грядет шестнадцатый год.

А я у вас—его предтеча;
я—где боль, везде;
на каждой капле слёзовой течи
распял себя на кресте.

hold in our fists
the driving belts of the worlds!

This led to my Golgothas in the halls
of Petrograd, Moscow, Odessa, and Kiev,
where not a man
but
shouted:
'Crucify,
crucify him!'
But for me—
all of you people,
even those that harmed me—
you are dearer, more precious than anything.

Have you seen
a dog lick the hand that thrashed it?!

I,
mocked by my contemporaries
like a prolonged
dirty joke,
I perceive whom no one sees,
crossing the mountains of time.

Where men's eyes stop short,
there, at the head of hungry hordes,
the year 1916 cometh
in the thorny crown of revolutions.

In your midst, his precursor,
I am where pain is—everywhere;
on each drop of the tear-flow
I have nailed myself on the cross.

Уже ничего простить нельзя.
Я выжег души, где нежность растили.
Это труднее, чем взять
тысячу тысяч Бастилий!

И когда,
приход его
мятежом оглашая,
выйдете к спасителю—
вам я
душу вытащу
растопчу,
чтоб большая!—
и окровавленную дам, как знамя.

1914–15

Nothing is left to forgive.
I've cauterized the souls where tenderness was bred.
It was harder than taking
a thousand thousand Bastilles!

And when,
with rebellion
his advent announcing,
you step to meet the saviour—
then I
shall root up my soul;
I'll trample it hard
till it spread
in blood; and I offer you this as a banner.

1914–15

Translated by
George Reavey

SALUTATION THE SECOND: Ezra Pound

You were praised, my books,
        because I had just come from the country;
I was twenty years behind the times
        so you found an audience ready.
I do not disown you,
        do not you disown your progeny.

Here they stand without quaint devices,
Here they are with nothing archaic about them.
Observe the irritation in general:
'Is this', they say, 'the nonsense
        that we expect of poets?'
'Where is the Picturesque?'
        'Where is the vertigo of emotion?'
'No! his first work was the best.'
        'Poor Dear! he has lost his illusions.'

Go, little naked and impudent songs,
Go with a light foot!
(Or with two light feet, if it please you!)
Go and dance shamelessly!
Go with an impertinent frolic!

Greet the grave and the stodgy,
Salute them with your thumbs at your noses.

Here are your bells and confetti.
Go! rejuvenate things!
Rejuvenate even 'The Spectator'.
        Go! and make cat calls!
Dance and make people blush,
Dance the dance of the phallus
        and tell anecdotes of Cybele!
Speak of the indecorous conduct of the Gods!

SALUTATION THE SECOND: Ezra Pound

Ruffle the skirts of prudes,
  speak of their knees and ankles.
But, above all, go to practical people—
Say that you do no work
  and that you will live forever.

1915

Biographical Notes

Guillaume Apollinaire (pseudonym for Wilhelm Apollinaris de Kostrowitsky, 1880–1918). Natural son of a Polish mother and an Italian father, Apollinaire made himself the central figure of his generation, as Mallarmé had been of his. He was a fervent and effective advocate of the Cubist painters who were his friends, and an eager promoter of every aspect of modernism.

Hans Arp (1887–1966). Perhaps better known as a sculptor than as a poet. One of the most important figures in the Dada movement.

Hugo Ball (1886–1927). Founder of Zurich Dada, which he later turned away from, on the grounds that it had not produced a real confrontation with the evils of society. Later turned to the study of theology.

Gottfried Benn (1886–1956). One of the few Expressionists to survive both world wars, Benn became the link between post-1945 German poetry and the modernist past.

Blaise Cendrars (pseudonym for Fréderic Sauser, 1887–1961). Cendrars's poetic experiments—with syncopated, Surrealist imagery, techniques derived from the early efforts of the cinema—give him a high place among the early modernists. He influenced Apollinaire.

Jean Cocteau (1889–1963). Cocteau's posturings have done a great deal of damage to his reputation as a poet. This 'fashionable' writer produced some of the best descriptions in French poetry of the experience of the First World War.

Stefan George (1868–1933). Like the other leading German Symbolist, Rilke, George was profoundly influenced by French literature. Because of his hermetic purism, attempts have often been made to deny him a place in the modernist movement, but in fact George is no less 'modern' than the Russian Acmeists, whom he precedes in point of time.

Richard Huelsenbeck (b. 1892). One of the original Zurich Dadaists, later responsible for the spread of Dada doctrines to Berlin. Delivered his 'First Dada Speech in Germany' in February 1918, and said in the course of it: 'We hated nothing so much as romantic silence and the search for a soul: we were convinced that the soul could only show itself in our own actions.' Huelsenbeck, who was a doctor, later emigrated to the United States.

Max Jacob (1876–1944). One of the most endearing figures thrown up by the modernist movement, Jacob was Jewish, but brought up in Catholic Britanny. These facts determined his life. He was an early associate of Picasso, and his little book *Le Cornet à dès* brought something entirely fresh into French verse when it was published in 1917. He died in a concentration camp at Drancy.

Velemir Khlebnikov (1885–1922). The boldest linguistic experimenter of his time in Russia, and the greatest of the Futurists next to Mayakovsky. Died of starvation in the difficult years after the Revolution.

Aleksei Eliseyevich Kruchonykh (b. 1886). Russian Futurist poet whose experiments were connected with Khlebnikov's.

Jules Laforgue (1860–1887). Laforgue's work represents a development both of Symbolist doctrines and of Symbolist verse-techniques. His *vers libre* was to influence many later writers. Much of his short career was spent outside France (as reader in French to the German Empress Augusta) so his full impact came only after his early death from tuberculosis.

Valéry Larbaud (1881–1951). Son of an extremely rich family, widely travelled, Larbaud is among the most elegant of the early French modernists.

Alfred Lichtenstein (1889–1914). An early Expressionist, civilized and urbane, killed in one of the early battles of the First World War.

Benedict Konstantinovich Livshits (1886–1939). One of the group of Cubo-Futurists which included Khlebnikov, Mayakovsky, and Kruchonykh.

Stéphane Mallarmé (1842–1898). The acknowledged leader of the Symbolists, Mallarmé influenced the development of poetry not only through his work (more difficult than any of the painting being done at the same time), but through his famous *mardis*—the Tuesday evening gatherings at his Paris apartment which influenced a whole generation of French writers. An important aspect of his poetry is the attempt to turn poems into self-sufficient works of art.

Anatoly Borisovich Marienhof (1897–1962). Member of the Ego-Futurists, who enjoyed a brief but considerable vogue at the time of the Revolution.

Filippo Tommaso Marinetti (1876–1944). As the inventor and promoter of Futurism, Marinetti caused an immense stir in the pre-war world. Later, his influence declined, and he died, forgotten, as a camp-follower of Mussolini.

Vladimir Mayakovsky (1893–1930). The most considerable of all the Futurist writers, and the most committed to the political Revolution. Despite his suicide in 1930, apparently in despair at the way things were going, Mayakovsky remains officially honoured in Russia as a revolutionary hero.

Christian Morgenstern (1871–1914). Morgenstern's burlesque poems, as opposed to his serious ones, represent almost the earliest emergence of modernist tendencies in German literature.

Wilfred Owen (1893–1918). Probably the greatest loss suffered by English literature in the First World War, Owen scarcely had time to do more than establish a unique literary personality before he was killed.

Ezra Pound (b. 1885). Emigrated from the United States to Europe in 1908, and settled in England in 1909, where he remained until 1920. Later went to live in Paris and in Rapallo. During his English phase Pound was one of the principal channels for modernist influence, where poetry written in English was concerned. He had a decisive influence both on W. B. Yeats (then in mid-career), and on his fellow-expatriate T. S. Eliot.

Pierre Reverdy (1889–1960). A close friend of all the Cubist painters—Braque, Picasso, Juan Gris and Gleizes—Reverdy has been labelled the 'poéte Cubiste' in France. In fact, there is in his work a fine balance between classicism and modernism.

Rainer Maria Rilke (1875–1926). The most considerable of the German Symbolists, later influenced by Expressionism. A restless traveller, Rilke was widely cultivated. He represents another version of the detached life of the artist.

Arthur Rimbaud (1854–1891). Perhaps the most astonishing literary figure of the nineteenth century, Rimbaud was writing major poetry at the age of sixteen. But his theory of the poet as seer or *voyant*, who arrived at truth through the 'dérèglement de tous les sens', proved a tragic failure when he tried to put it into practice in his own life, though it was to exercise a profound influence on modernist poetry. Rimbaud had renounced literature by 1877, and had embarked on an adventurous career which was to take him to Cyprus, Aden and Abyssinia.

Isaac Rosenberg (1890–1918). One of the few British poets of the First World War not to come from the middle class. After being apprenticed to an engraver, attended the Slade. Edward Marsh helped him with small sums of money, which enabled him to publish some of his poems. Often clumsy in style, but also profoundly original.

Kurt Schwitters (1887–1948). Again better known as an artist than as a writer—his chief works are his delicate collages. He laid great stress on his own poems, however. Schwitters' MERZ was a total activity which embraced all forms of art.

Gertrude Stein (1874–1946). From 1902 onwards an expatriate in Paris, where she knew most of the leading painters. Has received some credit for her influence on Hemingway, but is still not fully recognized as the most 'advanced' writer writing in English of the pre-war period.

August Stramm (1864–1915). Among the most radical experimenters with language among the German Expressionists. Killed in the war.

Georg Trakl (1886–1914). The best of the German Expressionist poets. Published two books of poems in his lifetime. An already unstable personality, he suffered a mental breakdown after he had been put in charge of serious casualties whom he could do little to help, after the battle of Grodek in Galicia. Died in mental hospital in Cracow in November 1914.

Tristan Tzara (1896–1963). The most brilliant and amusing of the Dada provocateurs, later much involved in the brawls that marked the birth of Surrealism. A prolific author of manifestoes as well as a poet.

Giuseppe Ungaretti (b. 1888). The earliest of the Italian modernists, apart from those who attached themselves to Futurism. Ungaretti is cosmopolitan. He was born in Alexandria, studied in Paris, where Apollinaire was one of his friends, and in later years taught in São Paulo. His poetry is influenced by the French Symbolists, notably Mallarmé and Paul Valéry.

César Vallejo (1895–1937). Born of middle-class parents, left his native Peru after being unjustly imprisoned. Subsequently lived in poverty in Spain and France. In his later years became a more specifically political writer, thanks to his involvement with the Spanish Republican cause.